MINIATURE WOODEN CLOCKS
FOR THE SCROLL SAW

BY RICK AND KAREN LONGABAUGH

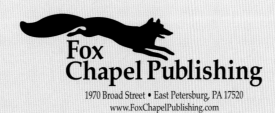

Fox
Chapel Publishing

1970 Broad Street • East Petersburg, PA 17520
www.FoxChapelPublishing.com

Miniature Wooden Clocks for the Scroll Saw is a compilation of projects featured in *400 Full-Size Mini-Clock Patterns* by Rick and Karen Longabaugh. The patterns contained herein are copyrighted by The Berry Basket. Readers may make three copie of these patterns for personal use. The patterns themselves, however, are not to be duplicated for resale or distribution under any circumstances. Any such copying is a violation of copyright law.

Bibliographical note
Miniature Wooden Clocks for the Scroll Saw is a revised and expanded republication o *400 Full-Size Mini-Clock Patterns*, originally published in 1994. This edition of the work includes expanded instructions for getting started along with full-color photos and full-color photos of a selection of the finished projects.

ISBN-13: 978–1–56523–275–4
ISBN-10: 1–56523–275–5

Publisher's Cataloging-in-Publication Data

Longabaugh, Rick.

    Miniature wooden clocks for the scroll saw / by Rick and Karen Longabaugh. -- East Petersburg, PA : Fox Chapel Publishing, c2005.

    p. ; cm.

    ISBN: 1-56523-275-5
    ISBN-13: 978-1-56523-275-4

    1. Wood-carving--Technique. 2. Wood-carving--Patterns. 3. Miniature wood-carving--Patterns. I. Longabaugh, Karen. II. Title

TT199.7 .L66 2005
736.4--dc22   0509

Printed in China
10 9 8 7 6 5 4 3 2 1

To learn more about the other great books from Fox Chapel Publishing, or to find a retailer near you, call toll-free 1-800-457-9112 or visit us at **www.FoxChapelPublishing.com**.

Note to Authors: we are always looking for talented authors to write new books in our area of woodworking, design, and related crafts. Please send a brief letter describing your idea to Peg Couch, Acquisition Editor, 1970 Broad Street, East Petersburg, PA 17520.

Because scrolling wood and other materials inherently includes the risk of injury and damage, this book cannot guarantee that creating the projects in this book is safe for everyone. For this reason, this book is sold without warranties or guarantees of any kind, expressed or implied, and the publisher and the authors disclaim any liability for any injuries, losses, or damages caused in any way by the content of this book or the reader's use of the tools needed to complete the projects presented here. The publisher and the authors urge all scrollers to thoroughly review each project and to understand the use of all tools before beginning any project.

Alan Giagnocavo
Publisher

Peg Couch
Acquisition Editor

Gretchen Bacon
Editor

Troy Thorne
Design

Linda L. Eberly
Jon Deck
Layout

Jon Deck
Cover Design

Rick and Karen Longabaugh started The Berry Basket and Great American Scrollsaw Patterns—their family-owned online and mail order company, specializing in unique and useful scroll saw patterns and accessories—in the fall of 1990. What began as one set of collapsible basket patterns became a complete line of full-size woodworking patterns and hard-to-find accessories.

Rick has been featured on the popular PBS show *The American Woodshop* with Scott Phillips and also on the cover of *Popular Woodworking* magazine. Many of their unique projects have been published in a number of woodworking publications, including *Wood* magazine, *Creative Woodworks & Crafts*, *Popular Woodworking*, *The Art of the Scroll Saw*, *Scroll Saw Workshop*, and Patrick Spielman's *Home Workshop News*.

To find materials and supplies for scroll sawing, contact The Berry Basket, PO Box 925, Centralia, WA 98531, 1–800–206–9009, **www.berrybasket.com**.

INTRODUCTION

Welcome to the wonderful world of clock making. Functional, decorative, and available in almost any theme imaginable, clocks have become some of the most popular projects to make on the scroll saw.

This book features a wide variety of projects from The Berry Basket's unique collection for the popular 1⅜" mini-clock inserts. These fantastic projects are great for gifts as well as for earning extra income. Precise patterns and easy-to-follow instructions will enable you to complete your project with professional results, and you'll also find some basic scroll sawing tips and techniques to get you started.

With so many options and designs, from wildlife-themed to country to Victorian-style clocks, we're sure you'll find just the right project to suit your needs.

GETTING STARTED

The following scroll saw tips and techniques are intended to get you started and on your way to scroll saw success. You will find these techniques helpful in completing the projects in this book as well as other scroll saw projects.

SAFETY TIPS

Always keep safety in mind as you are working. Below are some general safety guidelines to take into consideration before you begin.

- Use glasses, goggles, or similar equipment to protect your eyes.
- Remove any loose clothing or jewelry before you operate your saw.
- It is always a good idea to work in a well-ventilated area. Consider using a mask, an air cleaner, a dust collector, or any combination of these to protect your lungs from fine dust.
- Be sure that your work area is well lighted.
- Keep your hands a safe distance away from the blade.
- Don't work when you are tired or unfocused.

COPYING THE PATTERN

The patterns contained in this book are intended to be your master patterns. We recommend making photocopies of the project pieces and then using a repositionable spray adhesive to adhere them to your workpiece. This method of transfer is easier, less time-consuming, and far more accurate than tracing. Using a photocopier will also allow

Figure 1. Be sure to sand the workpiece before applying the pattern. You may also want to sand the wood lightly once you have cut the design and removed the pattern to eliminate any "fuzz" and to get rid of any glue residue.

you to enlarge or reduce the pattern to fit the size of wood you choose to use. Please note that some photocopy machines may cause a slight distortion in size, so it is important to use the same photocopier for all of the pieces of your project and to photocopy your patterns in the same direction. Distortion is more likely to occur on very large patterns.

PREPARING THE SURFACE

For most projects, it is best to sand the workpiece prior to applying the paper pattern and cutting the design (see **Figure 1**). For the projects in this book, start with 80-grit sandpaper, move to 120-grit, and finish with 220-grit. Once you've cut the design and removed the paper pattern, it may be necessary to lightly sand any glue residue remaining, along with any "fuzz" on the bottom side.

TRANSFERRING THE PATTERN

Using a repositionable spray adhesive is the easiest and quickest way to transfer a pattern to your workpiece after photocopying it. (These adhesives can be found at most arts and crafts, photography, and department stores. Pay special attention to purchase one that states "temporary bond" or "repositionable.")

Start by setting up in a well-ventilated area. Lightly spray the back side of the paper pattern,

Figure 2. Use "repositionable" spray adhesive to adhere your patterns to the wood. A simple glue box, made from a common cardboard box, helps to confine the adhesive.

not the wood (see **Figure 2**). Allow it to dry only until tacky—approximately 20 to 30 seconds. Then, apply it to the workpiece, smoothing any wrinkles if necessary.

One of the most common problems with using repositionable spray adhesive for the first time is applying the right amount onto the back of the pattern. Spraying too little may result in the pattern's lifting off the project while you are cutting. If this occurs, clear Scotch tape or 2" clear packaging tape can be used to secure the pattern back into position. Spraying too much will make it difficult to remove the pattern. If this occurs, simply use a handheld hair dryer to heat the glue, which will loosen the pattern and allow it to be easily removed.

SELECTING THE MATERIALS

Selecting the type of material that you will use is very important for the final outcome of your project. All of the projects in this book have been designed so that hardwoods, plywoods, or a combination can be used to create your work of art.

Hardwoods offer a wide variety of species, colors, and grain patterns; however, they are more time-consuming to cut, require more sanding, are more likely to warp, and are more expensive to use (see **Figure 3**). Generally, any of the domestic or imported varieties will work well—ash, maple,

Figure 3. Hardwoods offer a variety of colors and grain patterns that can enhance your projects. Shown here from left to right are catalpa, red oak, cherry, birch, black walnut, white oak, mahogany, and American aromatic cedar.

Skip Tooth Blades

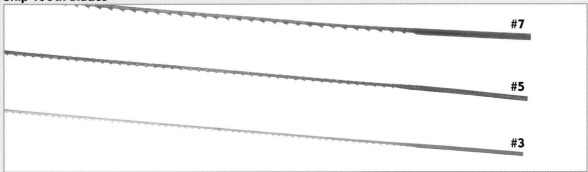

#7

#5

#3

Figure 4. Skip tooth blades can be good blades for a beginning scroller. Pictured here from bottom to top are skip tooth blades #3, #5, and #7.

walnut, oak, birch, mahogany, cherry, and hickory are just a few of the common types.

Plywoods, on the other hand, are less expensive, require less sanding, and come in a variety of standard thicknesses. They also are less likely to develop cracks or to warp. We do, however, recommend that you use top-grade plywood without voids, such as the Baltic and Finnish birches.

The patterns in this book have been designed so that a variety of stock thicknesses can be used, from ⅛" to ¾". For the majority of patterns, however, ¼" or ⅜" material would be ideal.

BLADE SELECTION

There are many opinions regarding which blade to use, depending on which type and thickness of material you choose and on how intricate the design in the project is. The more time you put into scrolling, the more your choice of which blade to use will become personal preference.

For the beginning scroller, we recommend skip tooth blades, but be sure to experiment and find the blade that suits you best (see **Figure 4**). We also offer the following blade size guidelines to get you started:

Material Thickness	Blade Size Recommended
¹⁄₁₆" to ¼"	#2/0, #2, or #3
¼" to ½"	#5 or #7
½" to ¾" or thicker	#7 or #9

SQUARING THE BLADE

Before you begin cutting, it's a good idea to check that your table is square to the blade. Lift the saw arm up to its highest point and place a 2" triangle or a small square beside the blade (see **Figure 5**). If the blade and the square aren't parallel to each other, adjust your table until both the blade and the square line up.

Figure 5. One way to check if your table is square to your blade is to use a small square. Place the square next to the blade and adjust the table as necessary until the blade and the square are parallel.

Figure 6. If you don't have a square, you can use a piece of scrap wood to square the table to the blade. First, make a small cut in the piece of scrap wood. Then, slide the cut toward the blade from the back. If the blade fits into the cut easily, the table is square to the blade.

If you don't have a square or triangle, try this method using a piece of scrap wood. First, make a small cut in a piece of scrap wood (see **Figure 6**). Then, turn the scrap wood until the cut is facing the back of the blade. Slide the wood across the table so that the blade fits into the cut. If the blade inserts easily into the cut, it is square. If the blade does not insert easily into the cut, adjust the table until the blade is square.

CREATING AN AUXILIARY TABLE

Most scroll saws on the market today have an opening in the table and around the blade that is much larger than what you need. This design often causes small and delicate fretwork to break off on the downward stroke of the blade. An easy solution is to add a wooden auxiliary table to the top of the metal table on your saw.

To make an auxiliary table, choose a piece of ¼" to ⅜" plywood that is similar to the size of your current saw's table. If you wish, you can cut this plywood to the same shape as the metal table on your saw, or to any shape or size you prefer. We do recommend, however, that you make the table larger than what you think you will need for the size of the projects you will make in the future.

Next, set the auxiliary table on top of the metal table. From the underside of the metal table, use a pencil to mark the location where the blade will feed through. Then, turn the auxiliary table over and drill a ¹⁄₁₆"- to ⅛"-diameter hole, or a hole slightly larger than the blade you will be using.

Finally, apply a few strips of double-sided carpet tape to the metal table on each side of the blade. Firmly press the auxiliary table onto the double-sided carpet tape, making sure that the blade is centered in the hole.

DRILLING

If you are going to use a 1⅜"-diameter Forstner bit to bore the hole for the clock insert, you must use a drill press. Drill the hole for the insert after attaching the paper pattern to the wood (see **Figure 7**). Be sure to clamp your workpiece to the drill press table for safety. Bore ¼" deep. If you don't have a drill press, use your scroll saw to cut the opening for the clock insert. After you attach the paper pattern to the workpiece, follow along the solid line to cut the 1⅜"-diameter opening.

Figure 7. Drill or scroll the hole for the clock insert after you have attached the pattern to the wood. If you are using a Forstner bit, you must use a drill press.

Figure 8. Drill any blade entry holes close to corners so that it will take less time for the blade to reach the pattern line.

Next, proceed to cut the outer shape of the clock, following the solid outside line.

If you have chosen to add a contrasting backing to your project, please refer to the procedures outlined in the Silhouette Backing section, page 8, at this time.

Now, drill blade entry holes where needed in the non-shaded areas. Sand the back to remove any burrs and proceed to cut the design portion of the project. When drilling blade entry holes, it is best to drill close to a corner, rather than in the middle of the waste areas, because it will take less time for the blade to reach the pattern line (see **Figure 8**).

VEINING

Veining is a simple technique that will bring a lifelike appearance to your project. The veins of a leaf or the folds of clothing will look more realistic when this technique is incorporated.

To vein, simply choose a thin blade (usually smaller than #7) and saw all solid, black lines as indicated on the pattern. You will be able to vein some areas of the pattern by sawing inward from the outside edge (see **Figure 9**); in other areas, you will need to drill a tiny starter hole for the blade.

If you wish to make a project easier, simply omit the veining.

Figure 9. Veining can give your projects a lifelike appearance. Many times veining areas will be as simple as cutting inward from the outside edge.

STACK CUTTING

Stack cutting is fairly simple to do and can save you a lot of time when you have two or more identical pieces to cut for a project or if you are making more than one of a particular project. If you are fairly new to scroll sawing and stack cutting, we recommend cutting no more than a total thickness of ½" for best results.

On projects with fairly simple shapes, two or three layers could be held together by double-

Figure 10. Small pieces of double-sided tape placed in the corners of the workpieces will secure the wood for stack cutting.

sided tape or by paper sprayed on both sides with glue and sandwiched between the workpieces (see **Figure 10**). You could also put masking tape on each edge of the stack to hold the pattern and the workpieces in place.

On more intricate projects, we suggest using #18 wire nails or brads that are slightly longer than the total thickness of the stack you are cutting. Tack the nails into the waste areas you will cut out, along with a few around the outside of the project. If the nail has gone through the bottom of the workpiece, use a hammer to tap it flush or use coarse sandpaper to sand the points flush with the bottom of the workpiece.

If you are stack cutting hardwoods, do not tack the nail too close to the pattern line or it may cause the wood to split. You could also predrill holes for the nails with a slightly smaller drill bit so the nail will fit snugly and hold the layers together securely.

SAWING THIN WOODS

Thin hardwoods or plywoods can be difficult to work with because they're prone to breaking. The

following suggestions should help to eliminate or reduce this problem.

- If you have a variable speed saw, reduce the speed to ½ to ¾ of high speed.
- If you do not have a variable speed saw, it will help to stack cut two or more layers of material to prevent breakage.
- For cutting any thickness of material, it is very beneficial to keep the fingers of at least one hand, if not both, partially touching the table for better control.
- Using a smaller blade with more teeth per inch helps to slow down the speed at which the blade is cutting. However, if the blade is leaving burn marks, you will need to slow the saw speed down or use a blade with fewer teeth per inch.

SILHOUETTE BACKING

For many of the projects cut from thin material, you can easily add a contrasting background, which beautifully enhances the appearance of the design (See **Figure 11**). This background offers versatility—it can be made from hardwood or plywood, and it can be stained, painted, or left natural.

Figure 11. Silhouette backing, or adding a contrasting background, can beautifully enhance the appearance of the design.

To use this technique, first saw the fretwork portion of the project, leaving the outer shape uncut until you are ready to glue on the backing. Use a painting or cosmetic sponge to apply a thin layer of glue to the back of the fretted workpiece. Center the workpiece onto the backing blank and clamp until dry. Then, simply cut along the outside line where indicated and use a ¼"R (radius) round-over bit if desired. Sand as necessary.

CHOOSING THE BASE

Several styles and sizes of bases have been provided on pages 116 to 123. This allows you to choose the style and size of the base to fit your particular project.

Just as you did with the other parts, adhere the paper pattern to the workpiece. Proceed by turning the workpiece on its side with the decorative pattern face up. Then, cut along the solid outside line.

FINISHING AND ASSEMBLING

When all of the pieces to a project have been cut, remove the paper patterns. Rout along the edges with a small round-over bit, if desired (see **Figure 12**). Then, sand any rough edges.

Assemble the clock by attaching it to the base and following any specific instructions given on the pattern pages. Where no specific instructions have been given for attaching the clock to the base, use one or more of the following after centering the clock on the base: glue, #18 x ⅝" finishing nails, or #6 x ¾" (or smaller) flathead wood screws. When you are working with glue, use it very sparingly and be careful that it doesn't run out. If you are staining your finished piece, any place where glue has squeezed out will not take stain. If you decide to use wood screws, drill and countersink the holes before inserting the screws. Predrill the holes for the nails.

Allow any glue to dry before finishing with a penetrating oil, such as Danish oil, Minwax Antique Oil Finish, or tung oil. An easy method of finishing using oil is to pour the oil into a shallow pan and soak the project for approximately 30 seconds (see **Figure 13**). Then, follow the oil manufacturer's directions. When the finish is dry, insert the clock.

INSERTING THE CLOCK

If you used your scroll saw to cut the hole for the clock and you find that, upon inserting the clock, the opening is slightly too big, try placing a thin rubber band, masking tape, or other material around the insert to take up the slack.

Figure 12. Use a router with a small round-over bit to round the edges of your project.

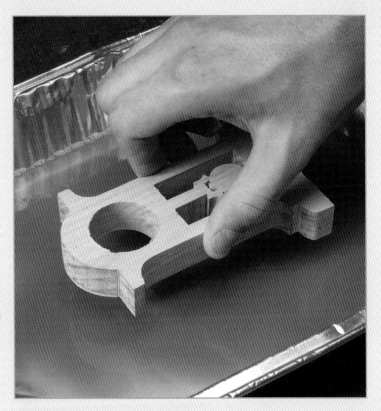

Figure 13. If you have used hardwood for your project, an easy method of finishing is to dip it in a dishpan or a similar container filled with a penetrating oil.

CHILDREN

NOTE: Several styles and sizes of bases are provided on pages 116 to 123 so that you can choose bases to fit your particular projects.

CHILDREN

CHILDREN

CHILDREN

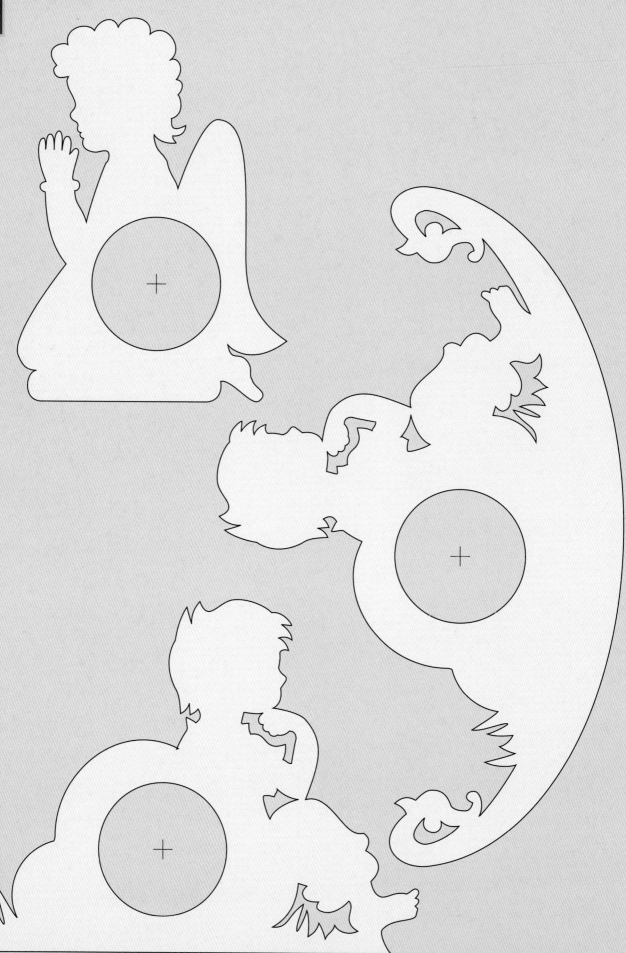

COUNTRY

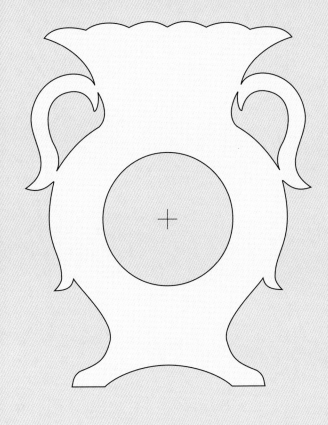

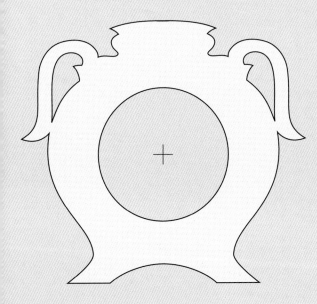

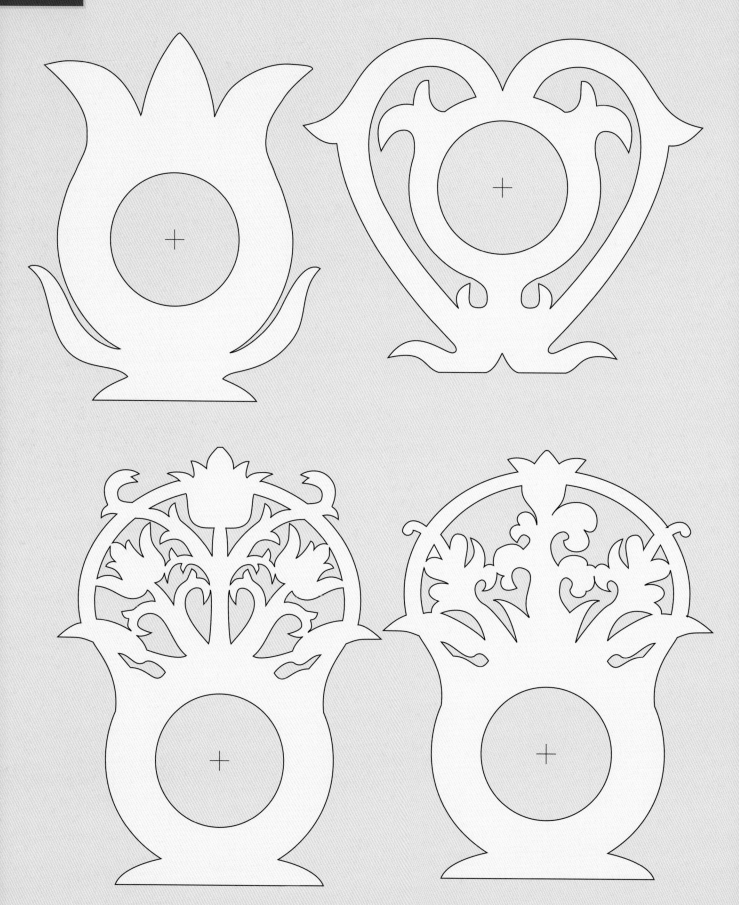

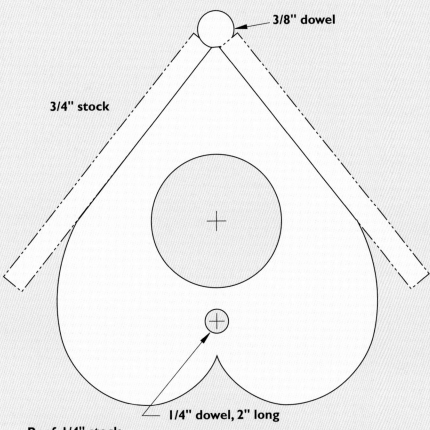

3/8" dowel

3/4" stock

1/4" dowel, 2" long

**Roof, 1/4" stock
cut 2**

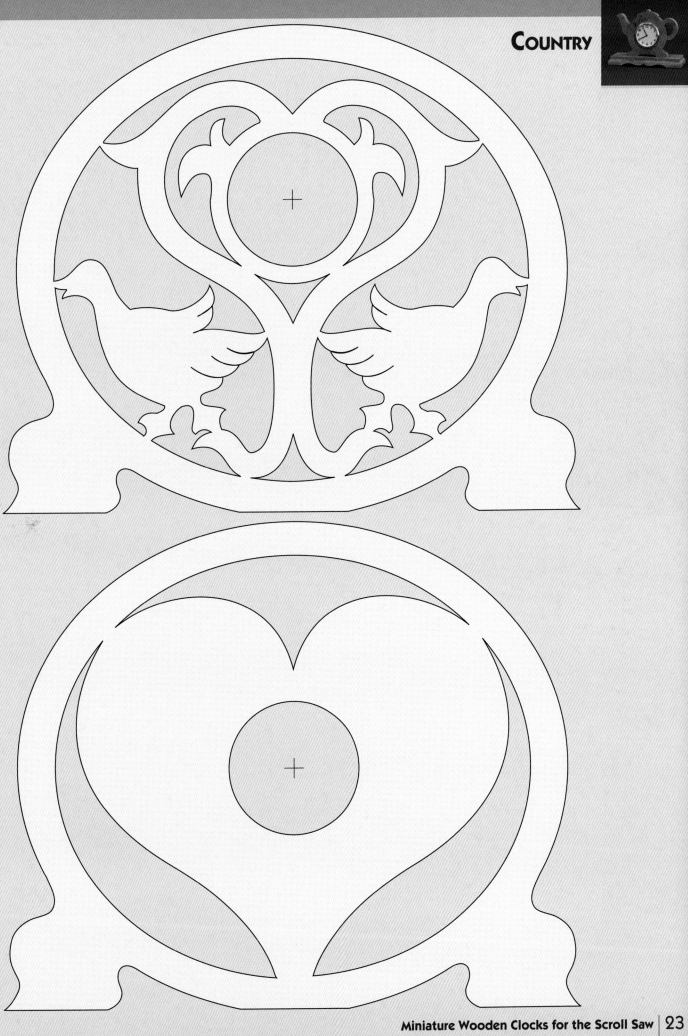

COUNTRY

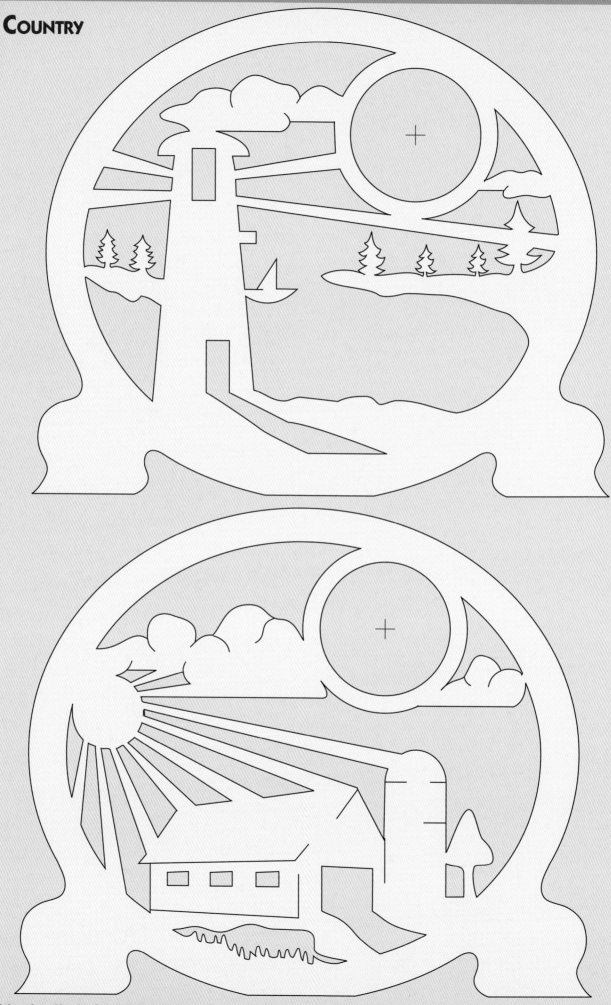

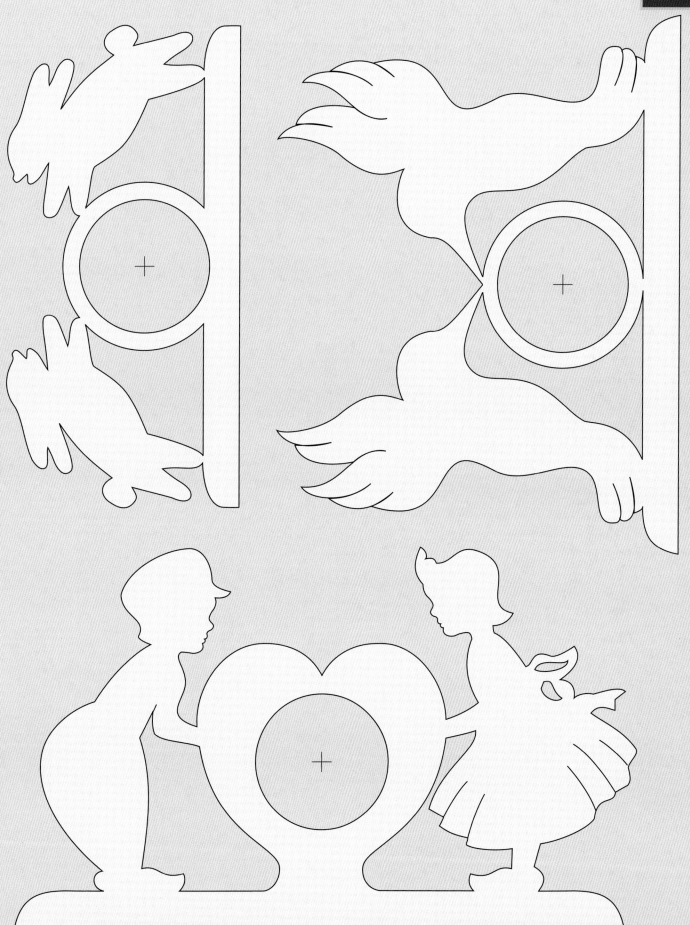

COUNTRY

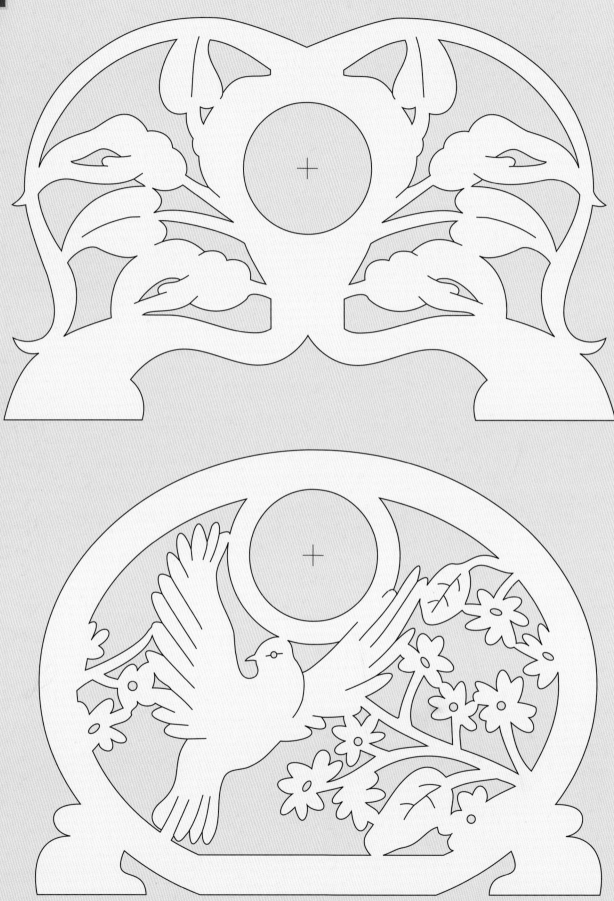

FANTASY

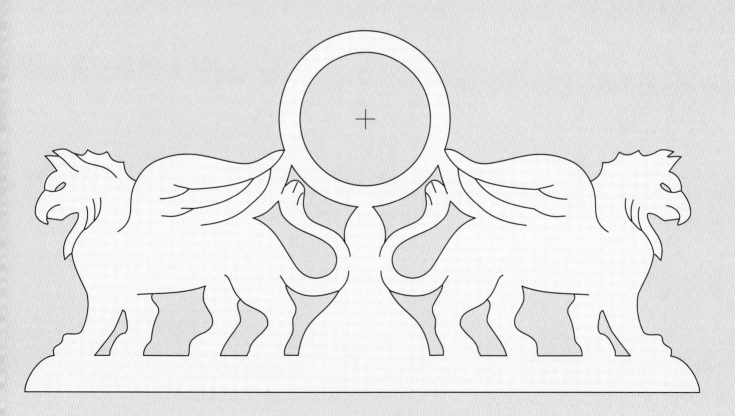

Fantasy

ANIMALS AND FIGURES

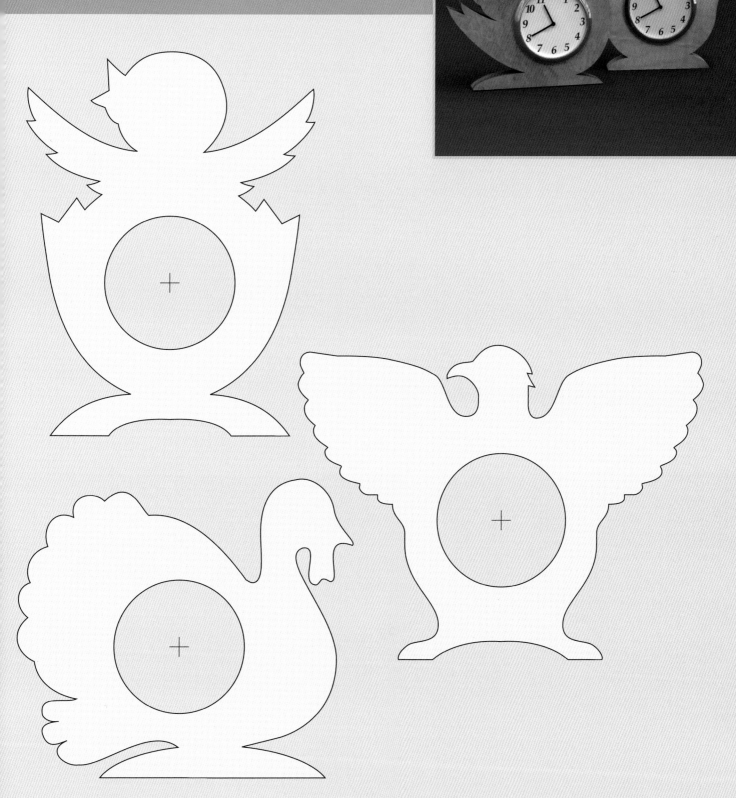

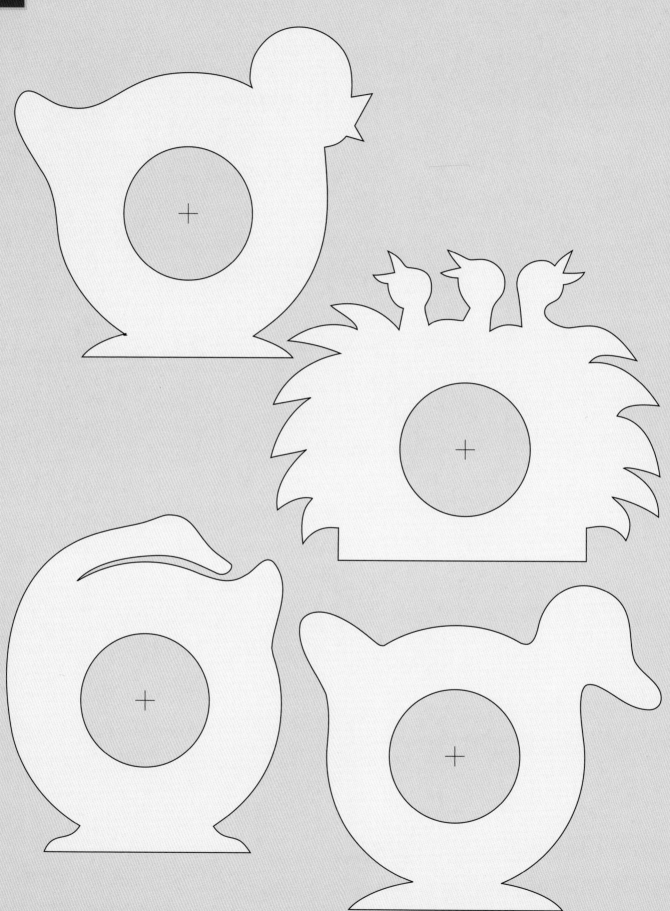

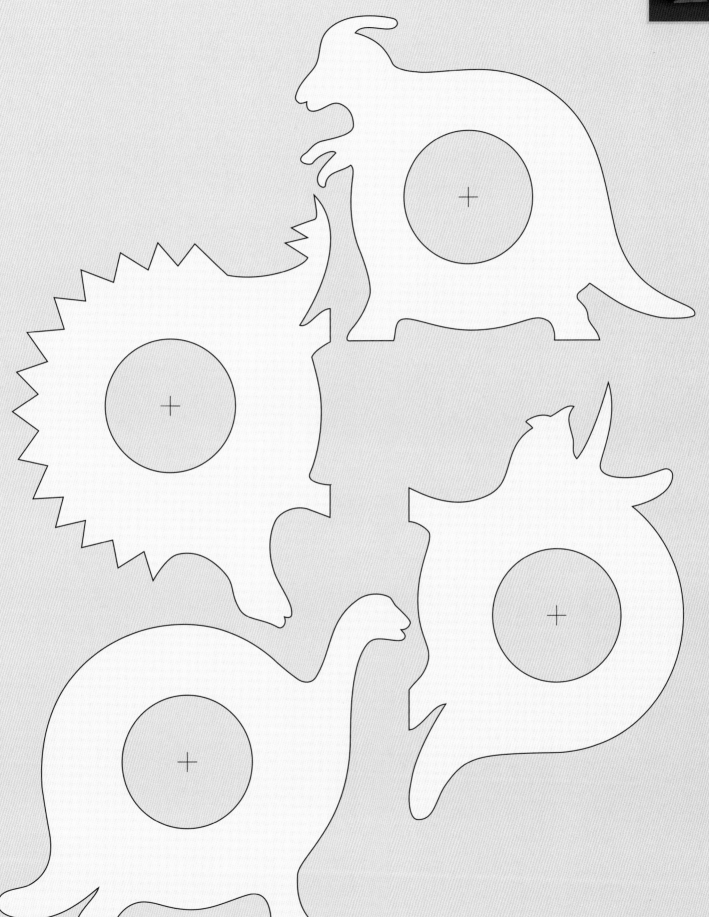

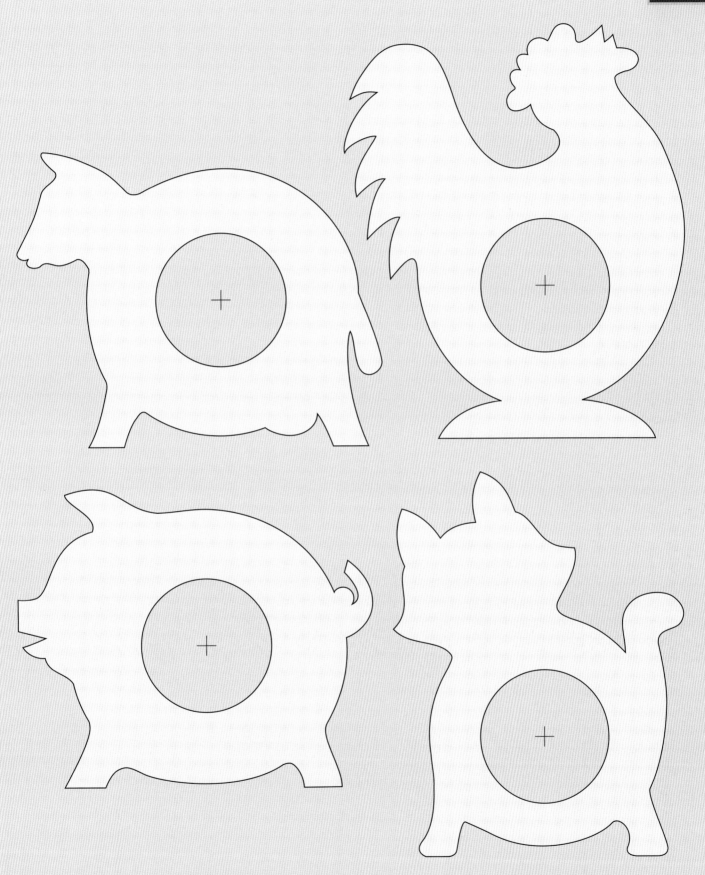

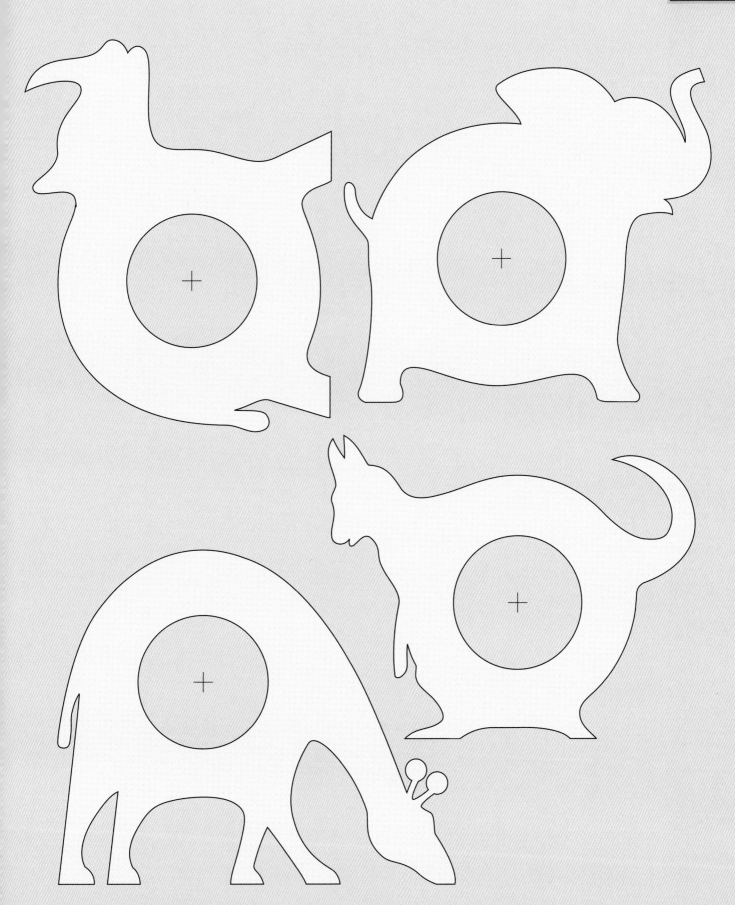

ANIMALS AND FIGURES

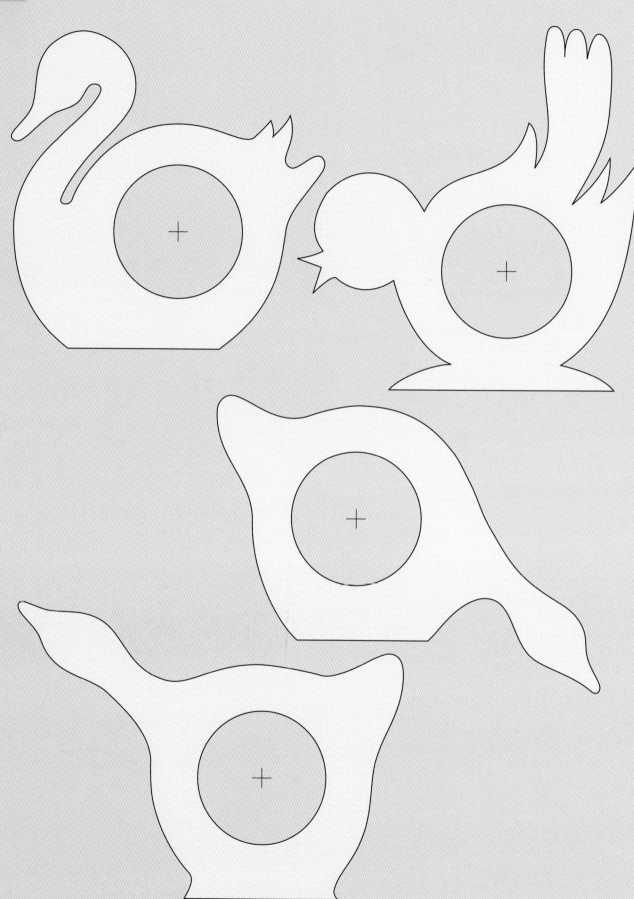

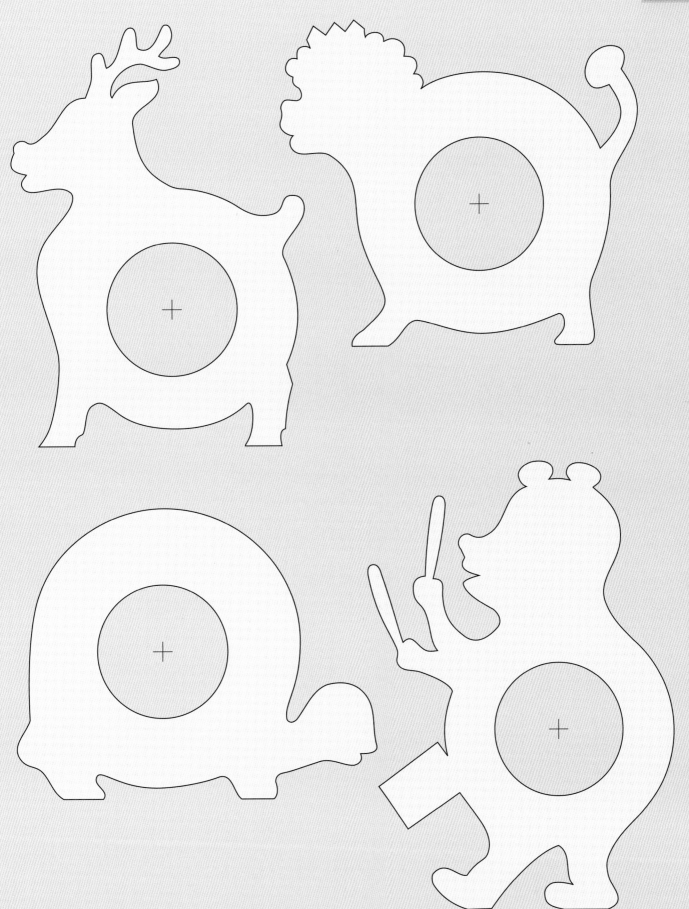

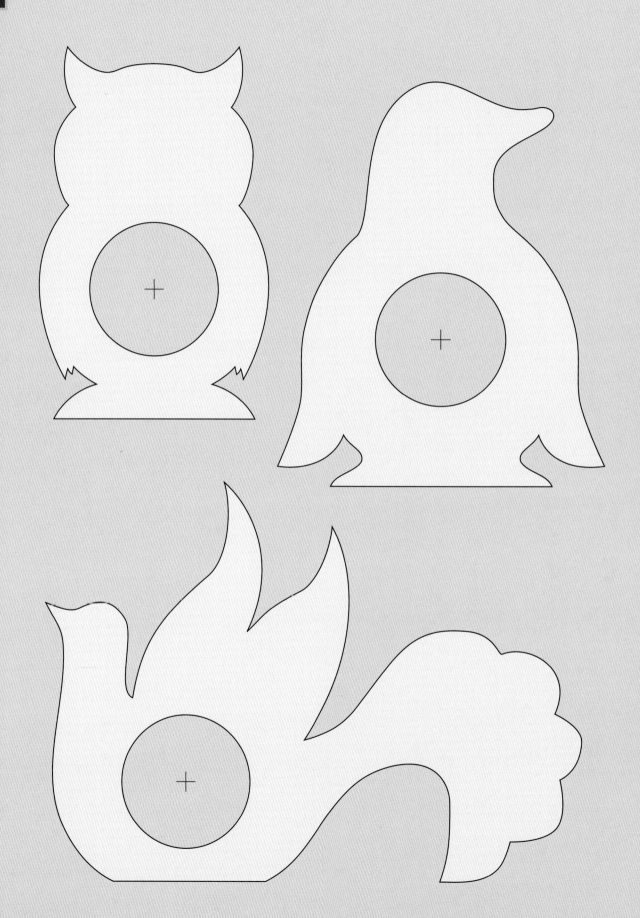

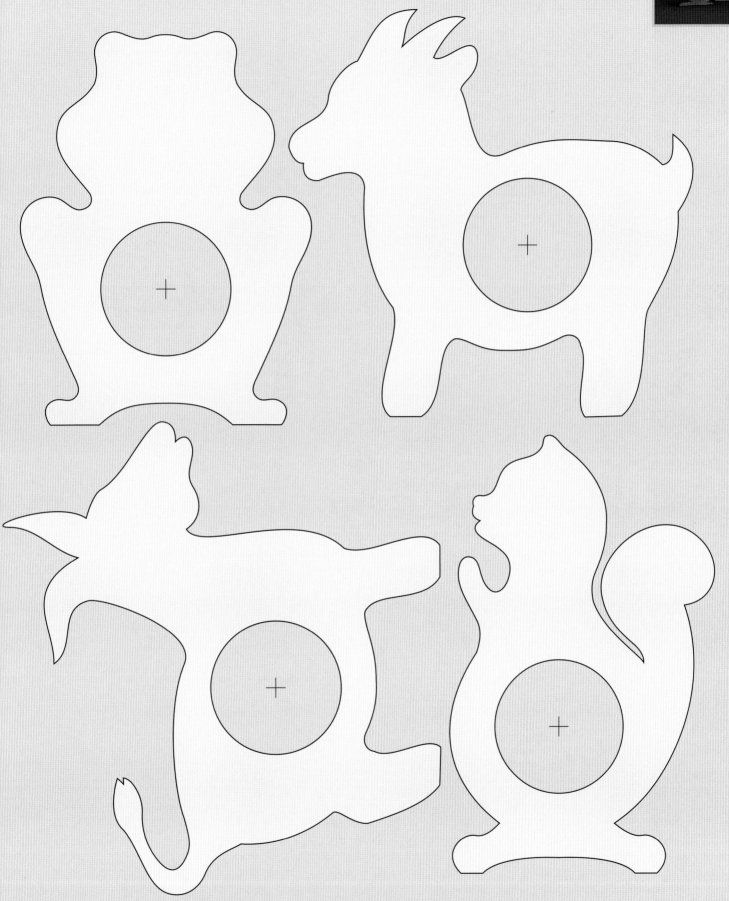

ANIMALS AND FIGURES

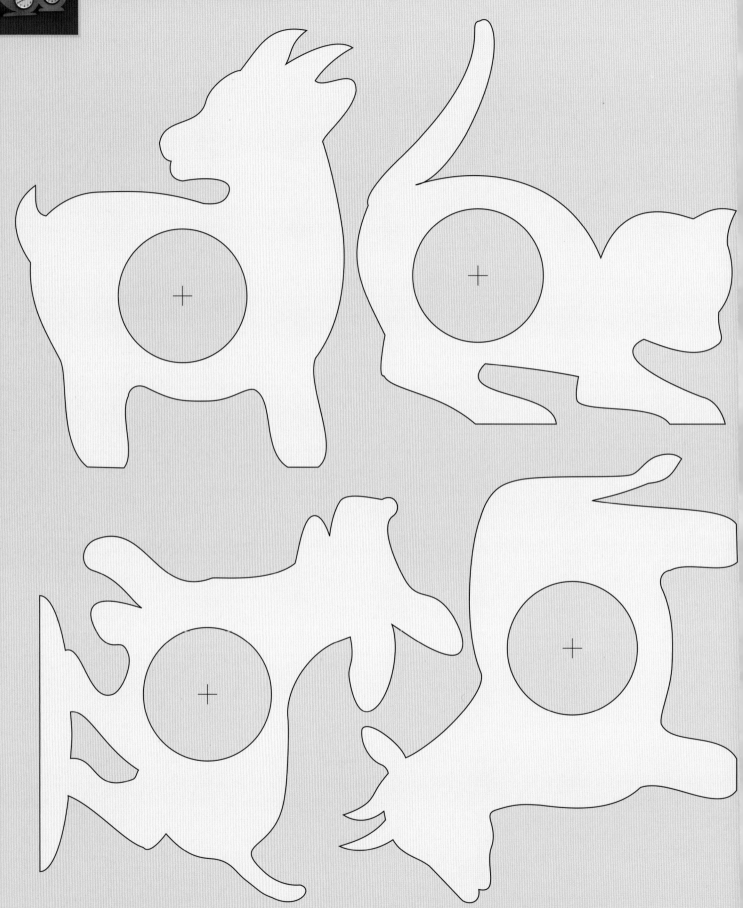

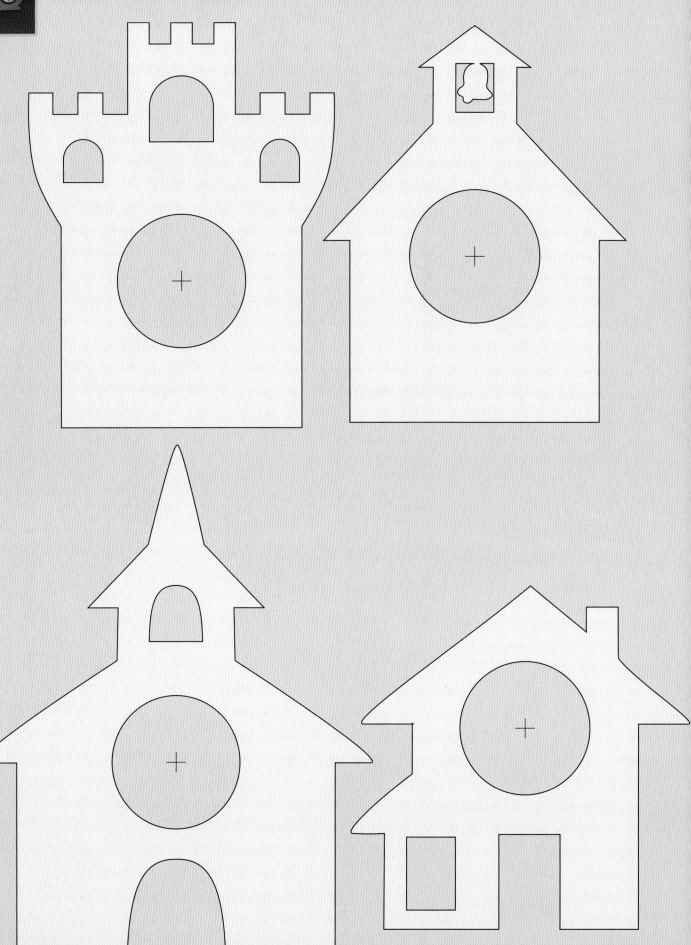

VEHICLES

VEHICLES

VEHICLES

Marine

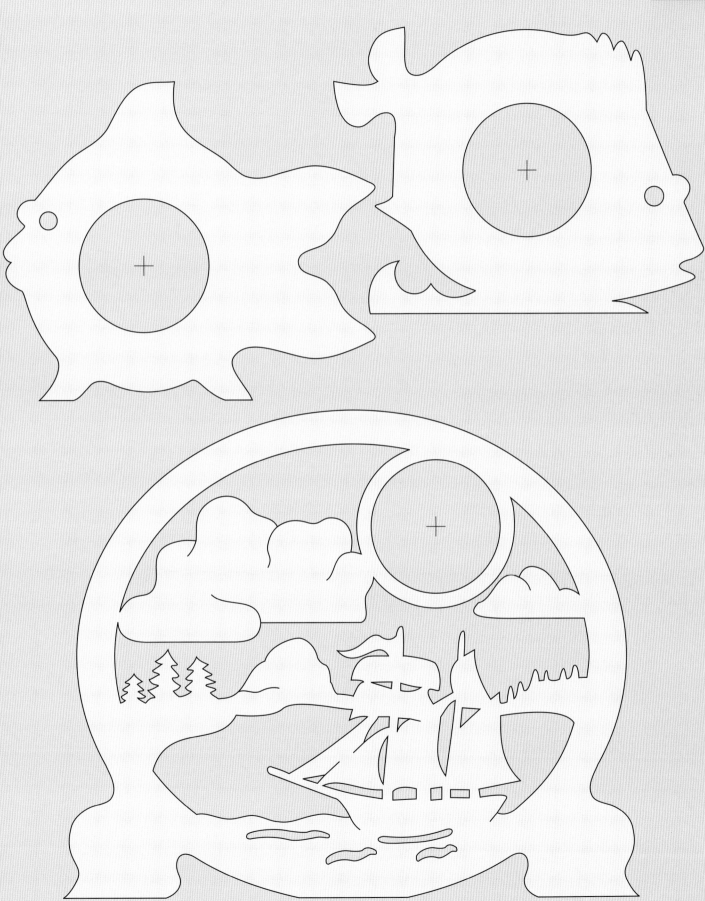

RELIGIOUS

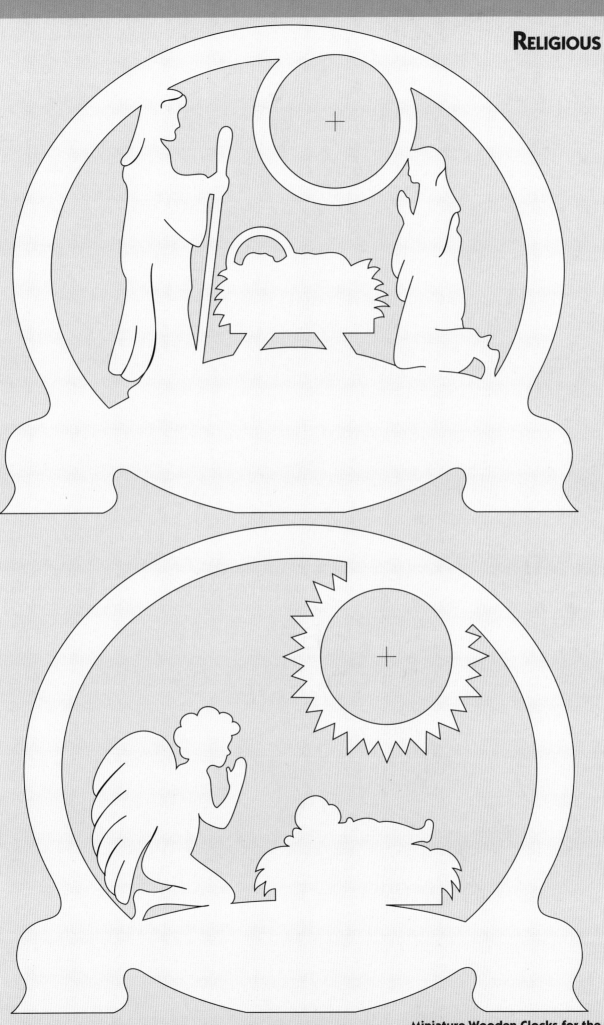

VICTORIAN

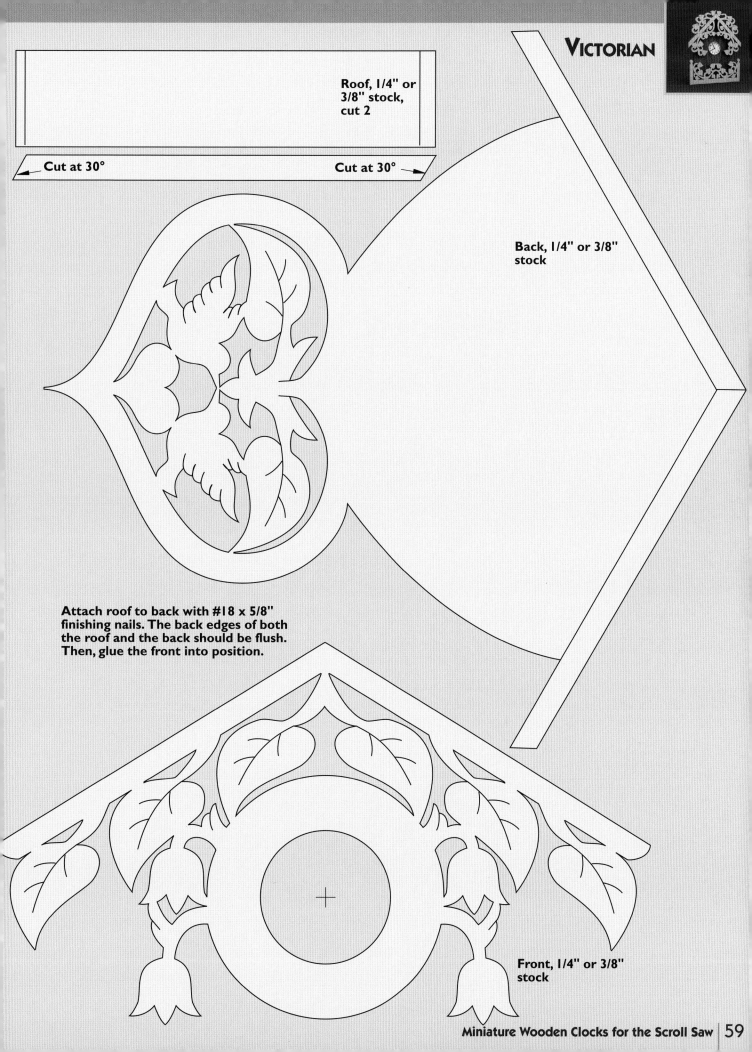

Roof, 1/4" or 3/8" stock, cut 2

Cut at 30°   Cut at 30°

Back, 1/4" or 3/8" stock

Attach roof to back with #18 x 5/8" finishing nails. The back edges of both the roof and the back should be flush. Then, glue the front into position.

Front, 1/4" or 3/8" stock

Front, 1/4" stock

Attach to roof with glue and #18 x 5/8" finishing nails.

Rail, 1/4" stock

Attach to front of base with glue and #18 x 5/8" finishing nails.

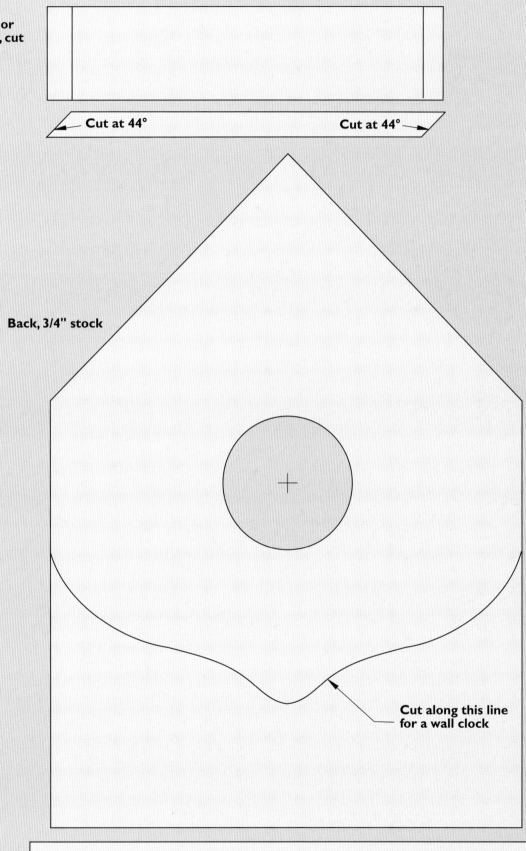

Roof, 1/4" or 3/8" stock, cut 2

← Cut at 44°   Cut at 44° →

Back, 3/4" stock

Cut along this line for a wall clock

Base, 3/8" stock

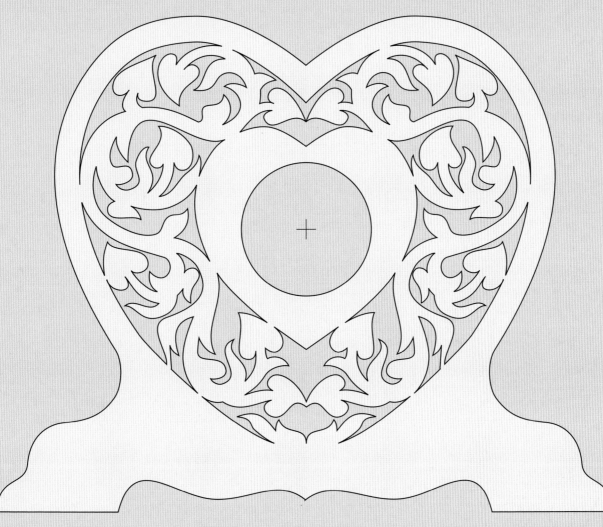

VICTORIAN

WILDLIFE

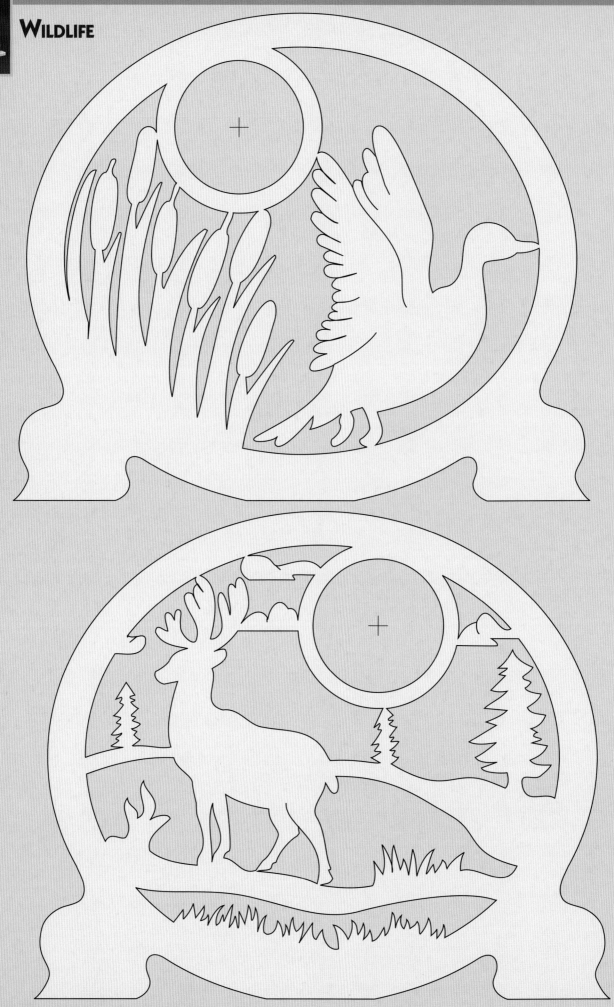

SOUTHWEST

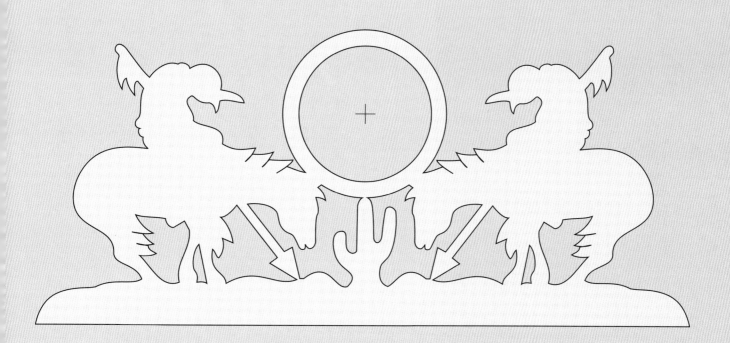

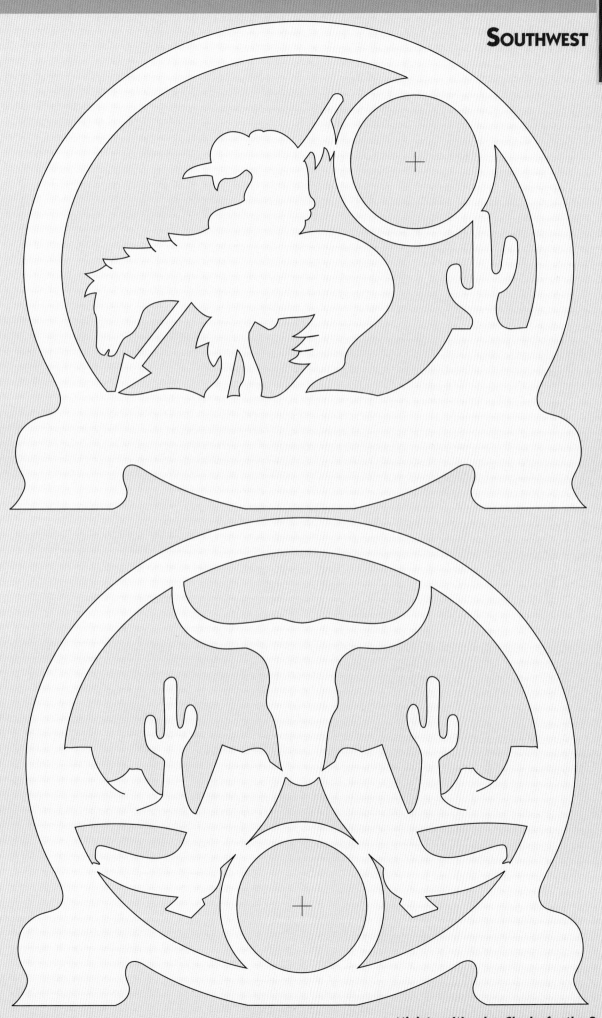

SPORTS

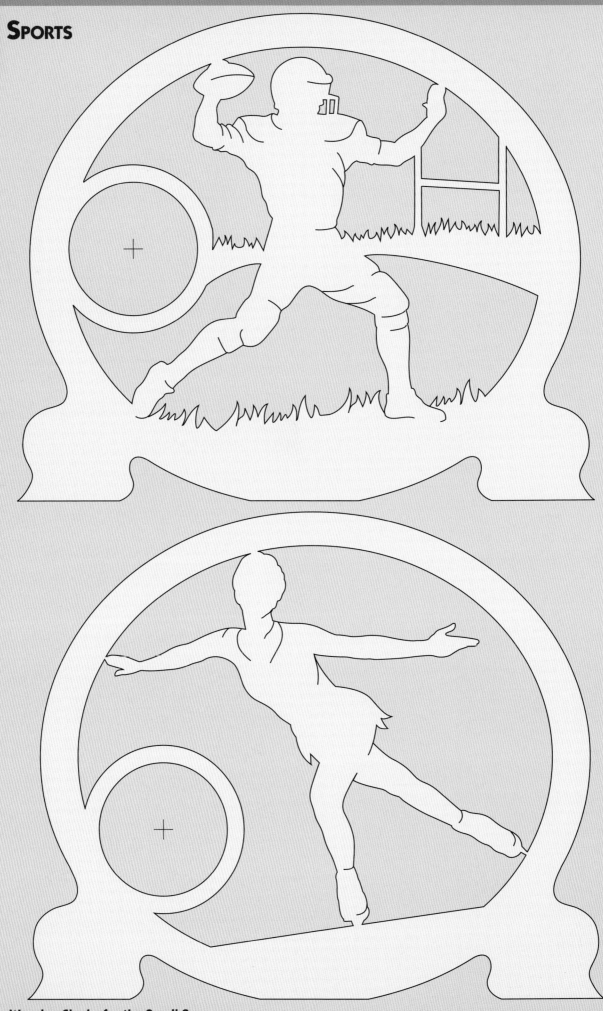

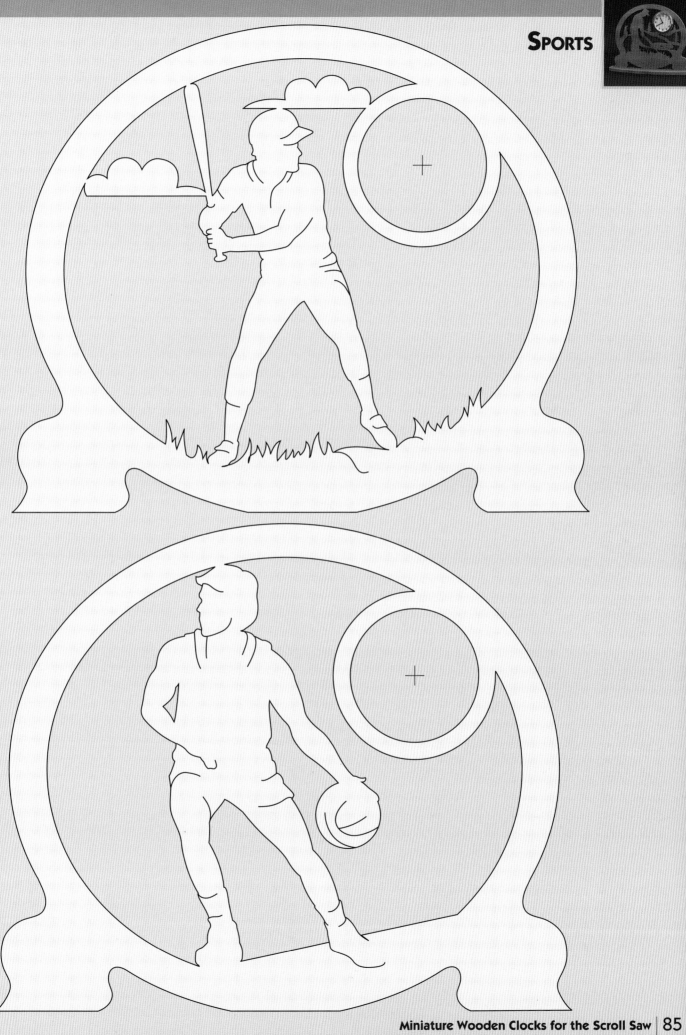

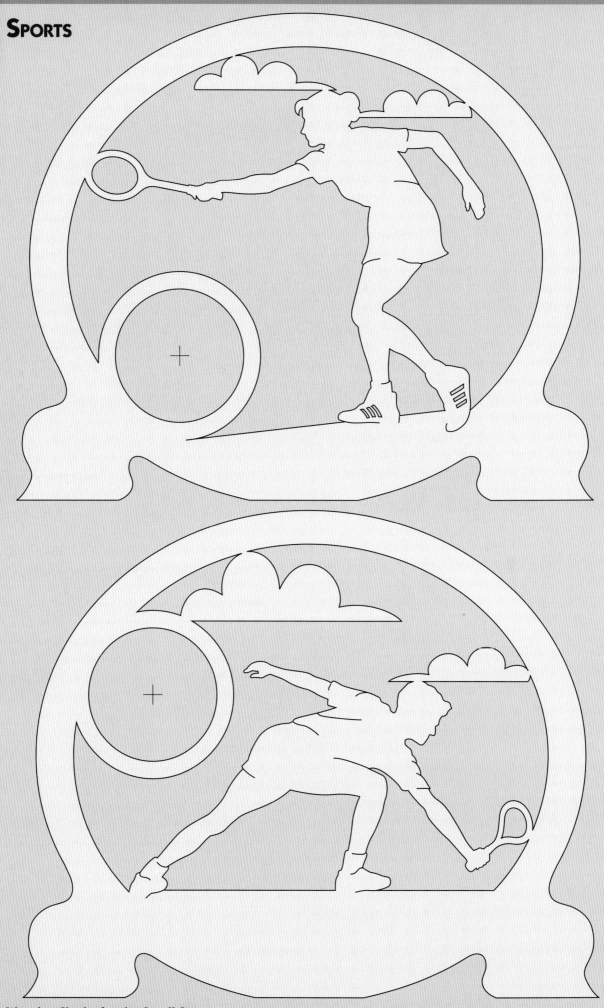

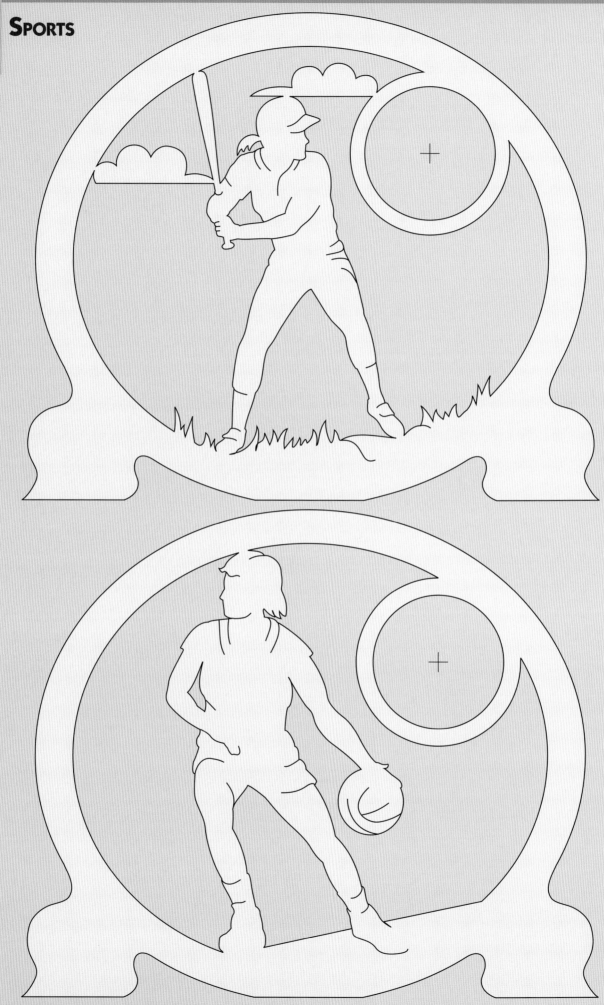

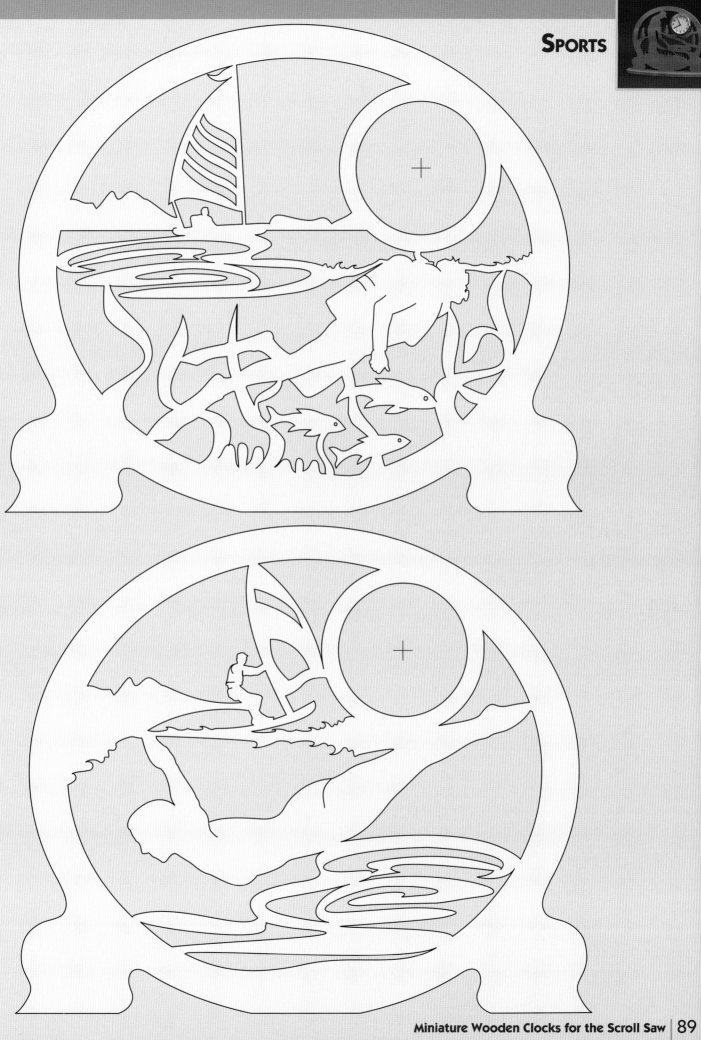

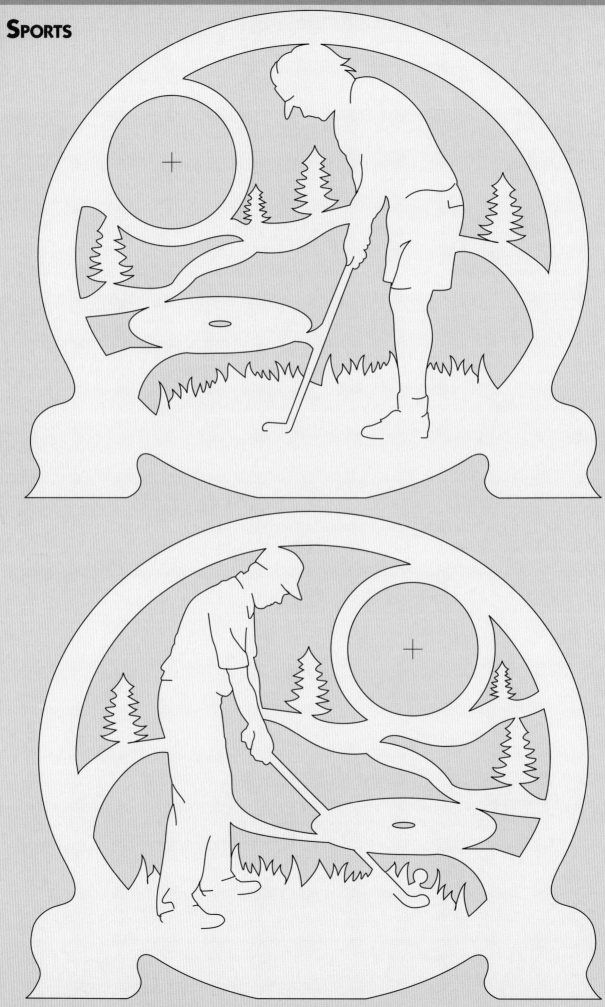

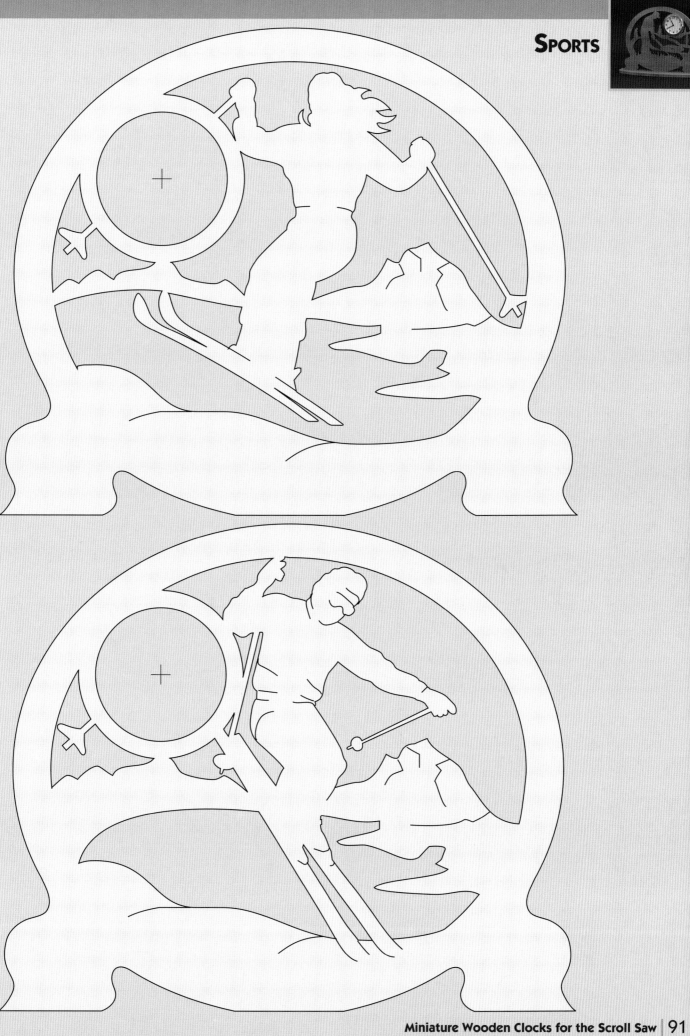

EXECUTIVE

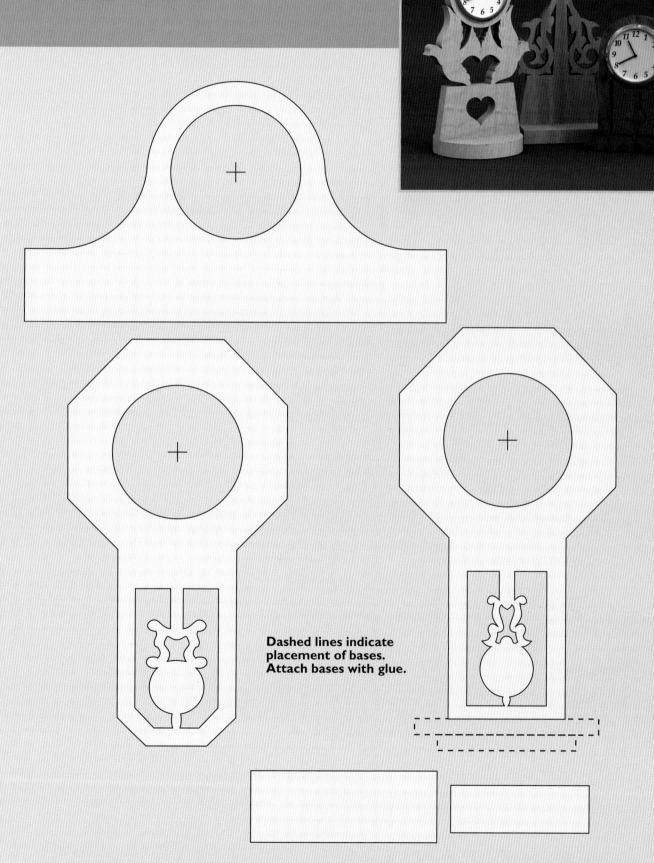

Dashed lines indicate
placement of bases.
Attach bases with glue.

EXECUTIVE

Frame and base, 3/8" stock

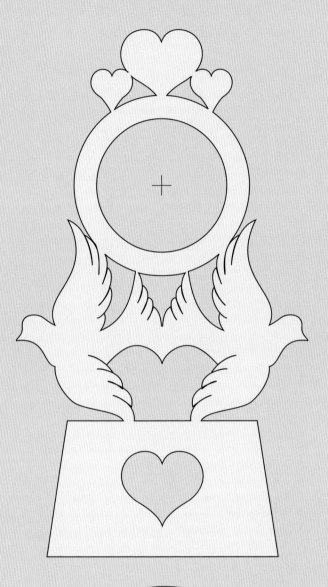

+

+

Attach frame here

Attach frame here

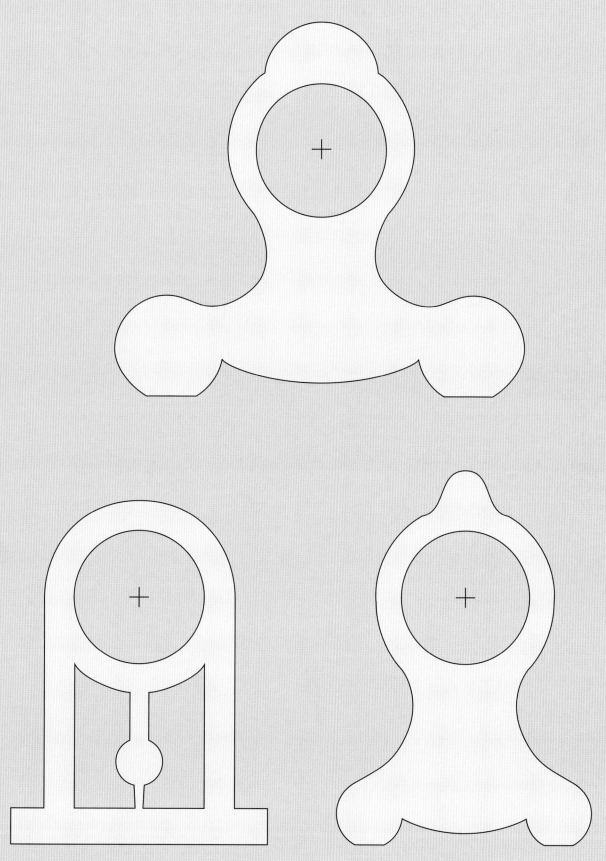

EXECUTIVE

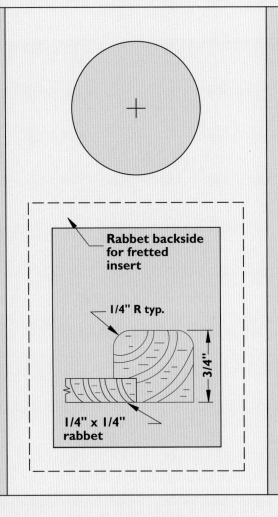

**Frame,
3/4"
stock**

**Rabbet backside
for fretted
insert**

1/4" R typ.

3/4"

**1/4" x 1/4"
rabbet**

**Top / Base, 3/8" stock
Cut 1 each**

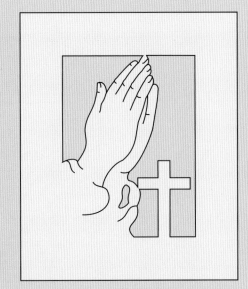

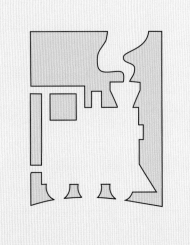

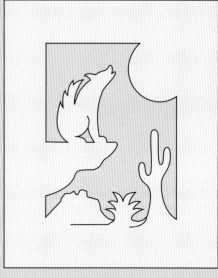

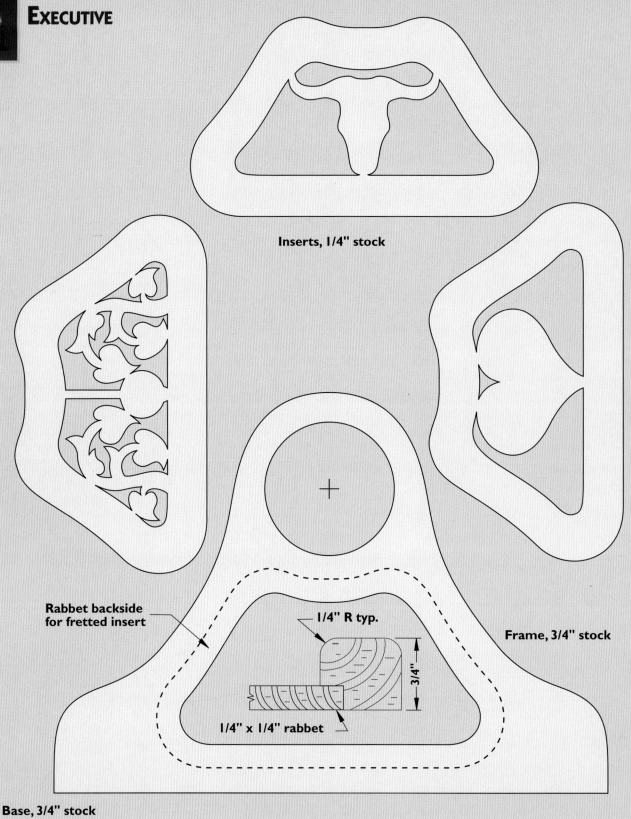

Inserts, 1/4" stock

Rabbet backside
for fretted insert

1/4" R typ.

Frame, 3/4" stock

3/4"

1/4" x 1/4" rabbet

Base, 3/4" stock

BUSINESS CARD HOLDERS

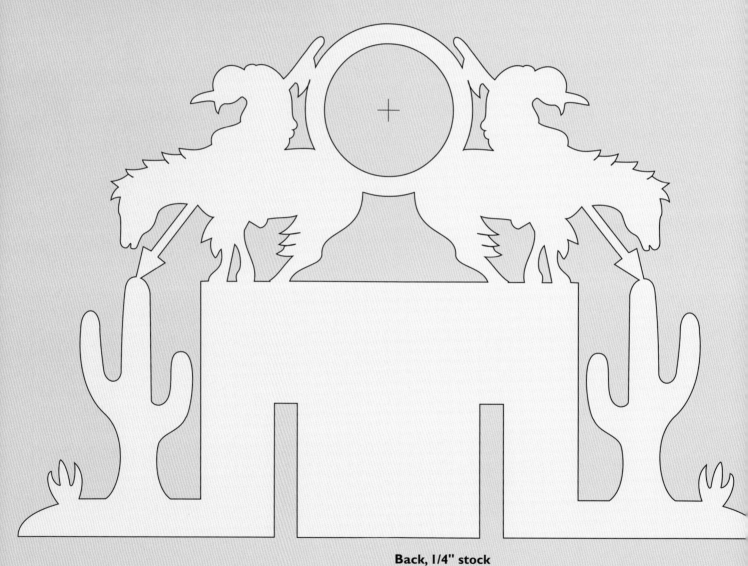

Back, 1/4" stock

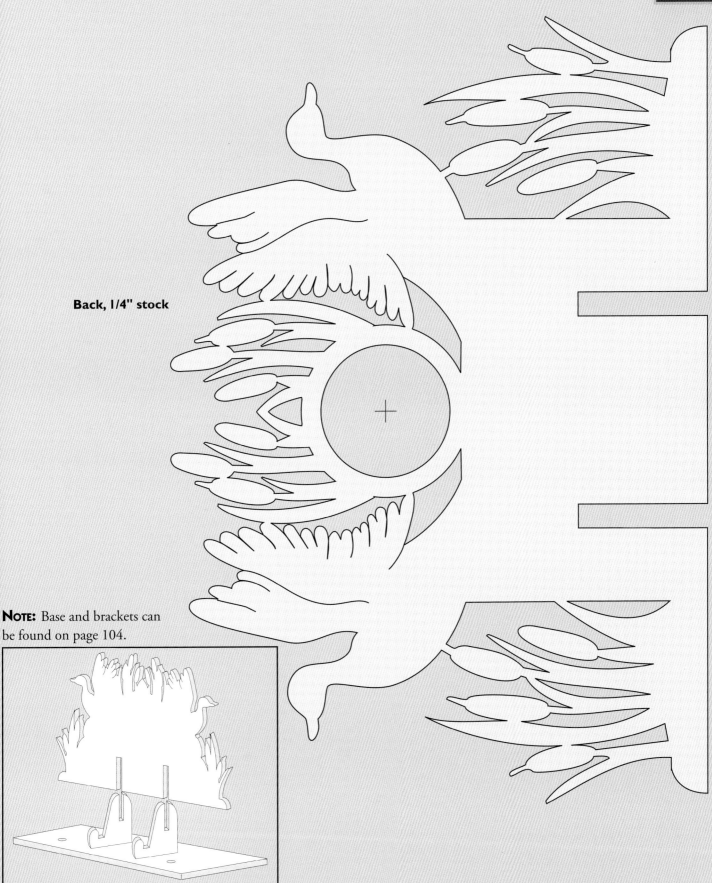

Back, 1/4" stock

NOTE: Base and brackets can be found on page 104.

Back, 1/4" stock

Back, 1/4" stock

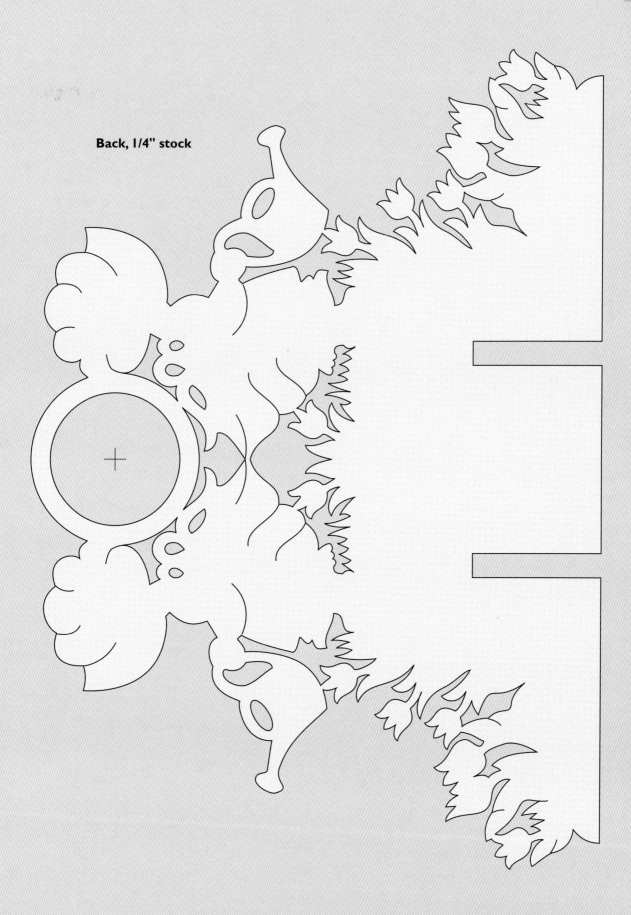

BUSINESS CARD HOLDERS

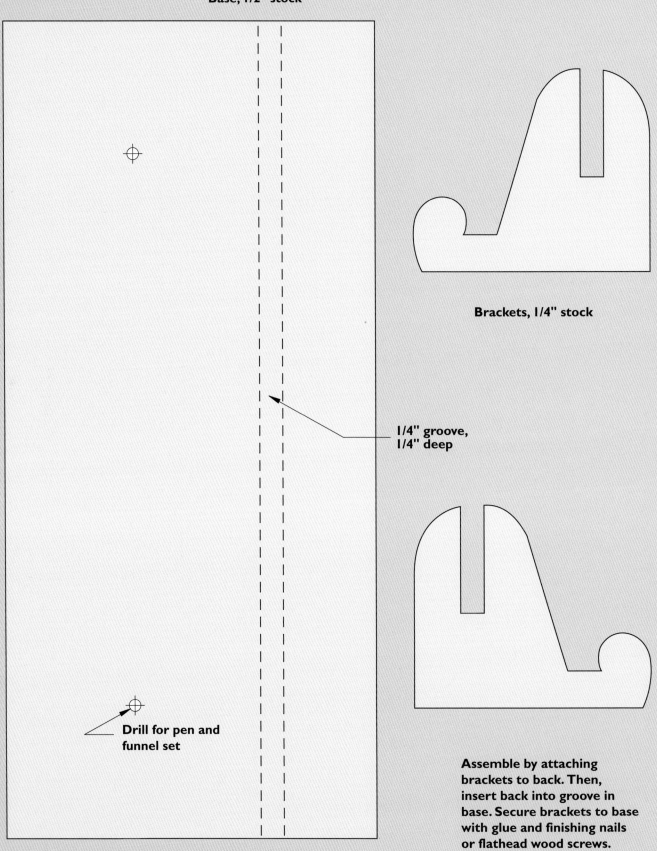

Base, 1/2" stock

Brackets, 1/4" stock

1/4" groove,
1/4" deep

Drill for pen and
funnel set

Assemble by attaching
brackets to back. Then,
insert back into groove in
base. Secure brackets to base
with glue and finishing nails
or flathead wood screws.

WEATHER VANES

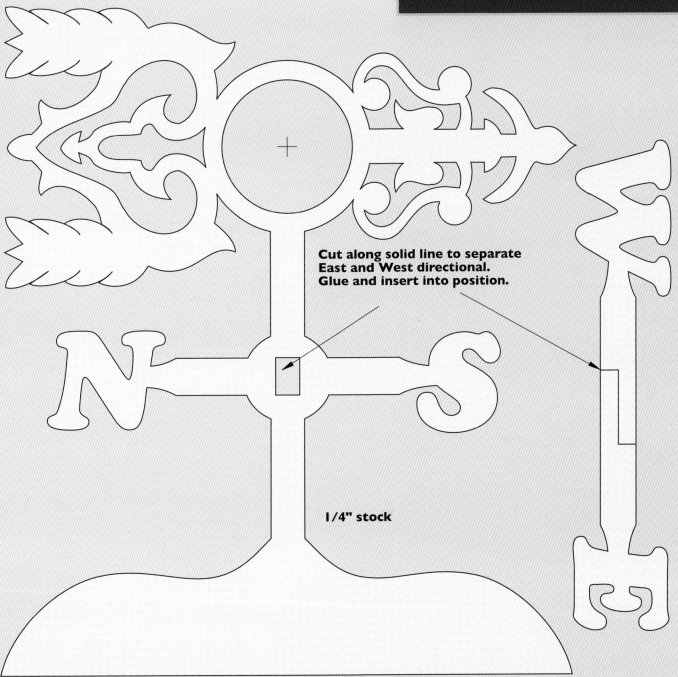

Cut along solid line to separate
East and West directional.
Glue and insert into position.

1/4" stock

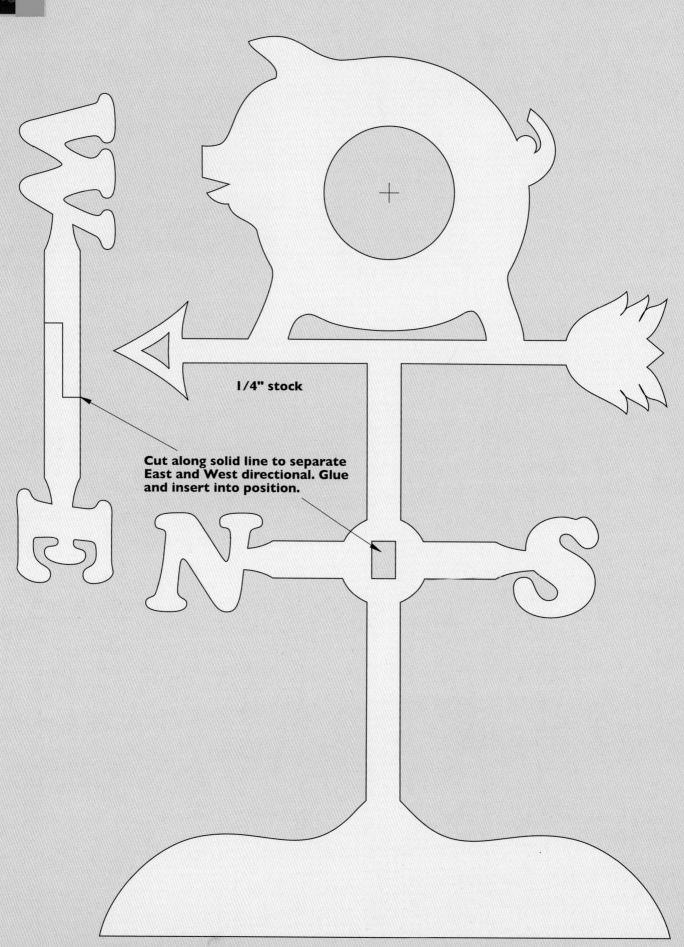

1/4" stock

Cut along solid line to separate
East and West directional. Glue
and insert into position.

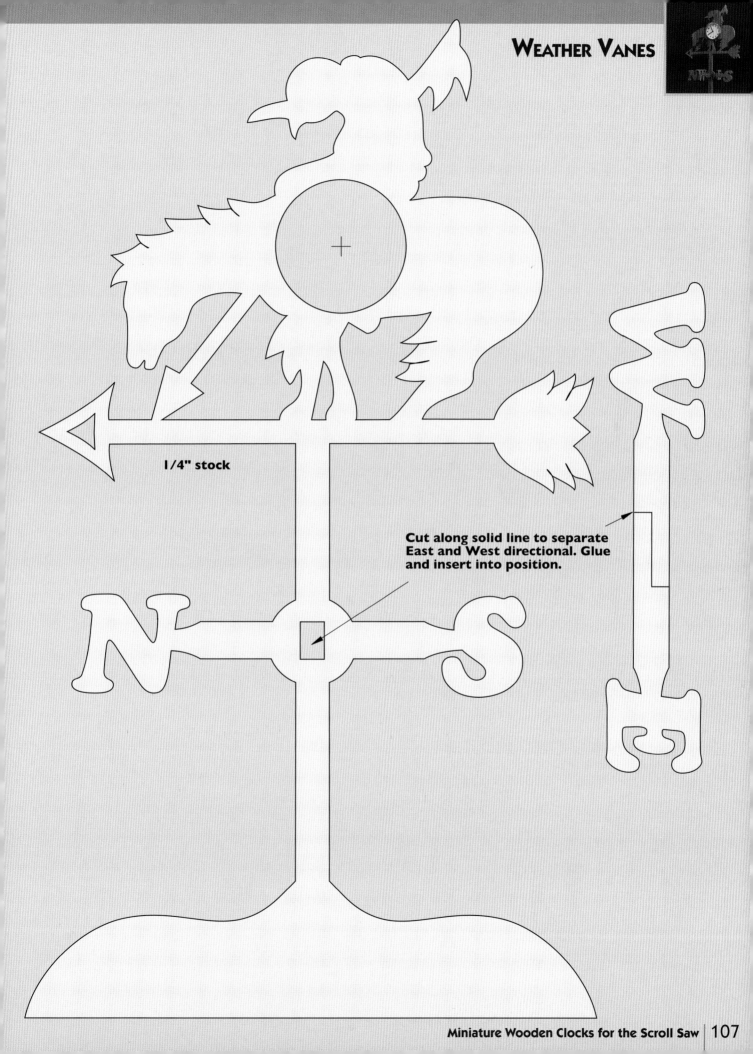

1/4" stock

Cut along solid line to separate
East and West directional. Glue
and insert into position.

1/4" stock

Cut along solid line to
separate East and West
directional. Glue and
insert into position.

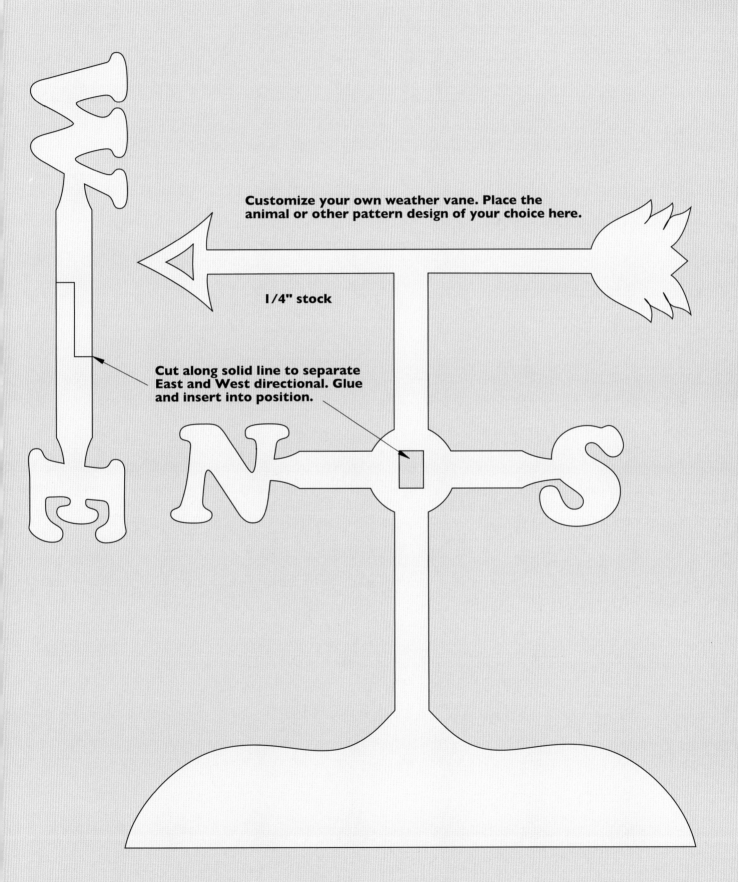

Customize your own weather vane. Place the animal or other pattern design of your choice here.

1/4" stock

Cut along solid line to separate East and West directional. Glue and insert into position.

ANIMAL CARTS

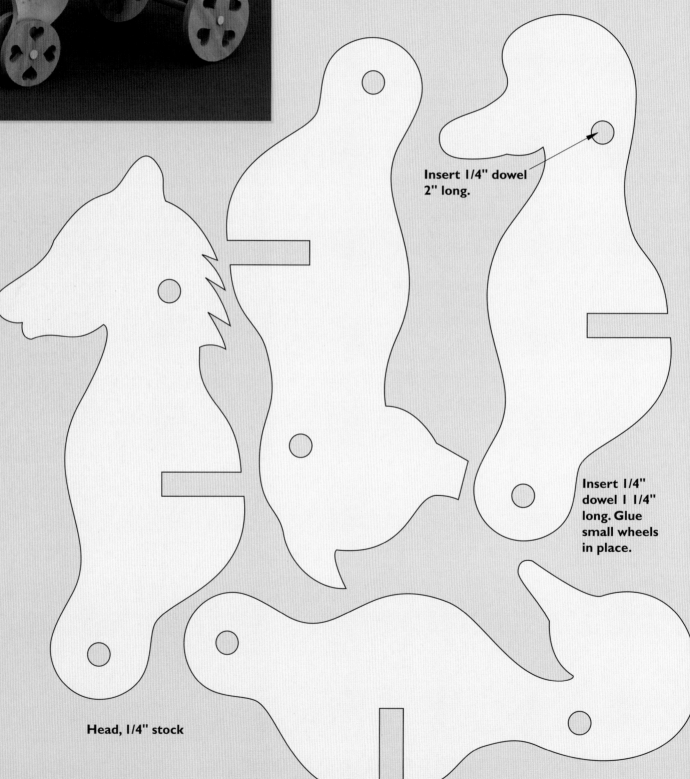

Insert 1/4" dowel 2" long.

Insert 1/4" dowel 1 1/4" long. Glue small wheels in place.

Head, 1/4" stock

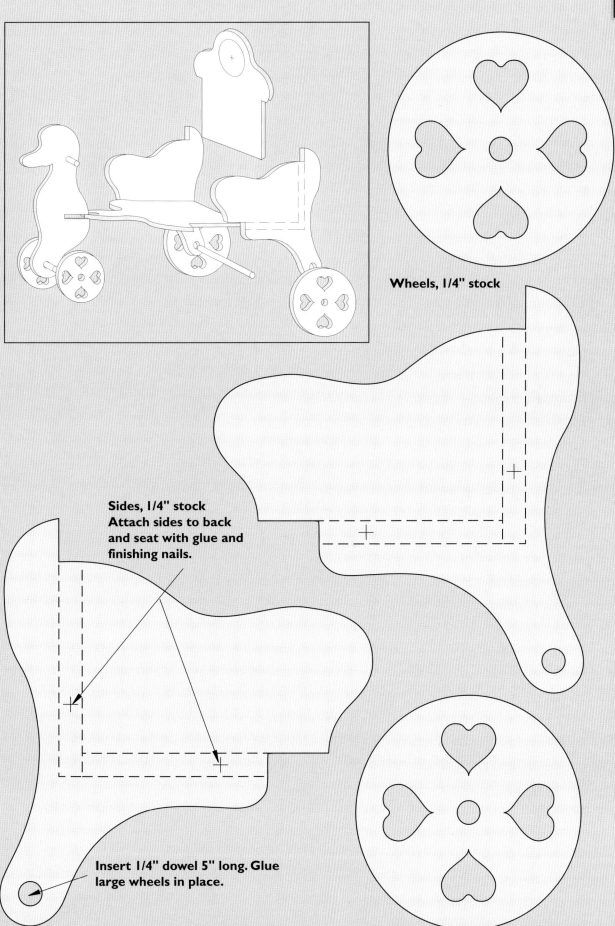

Wheels, 1/4" stock

Sides, 1/4" stock
Attach sides to back
and seat with glue and
finishing nails.

Insert 1/4" dowel 5" long. Glue
large wheels in place.

Animal Carts

Wheels, 1/4" stock

Back, 1/4" stock

Head, 1/4" stock

Insert 1/4" dowel 2" long.

Seat, 1/4" stock

Insert 1/4" dowel 1 1/4" long. Glue small wheels in place.

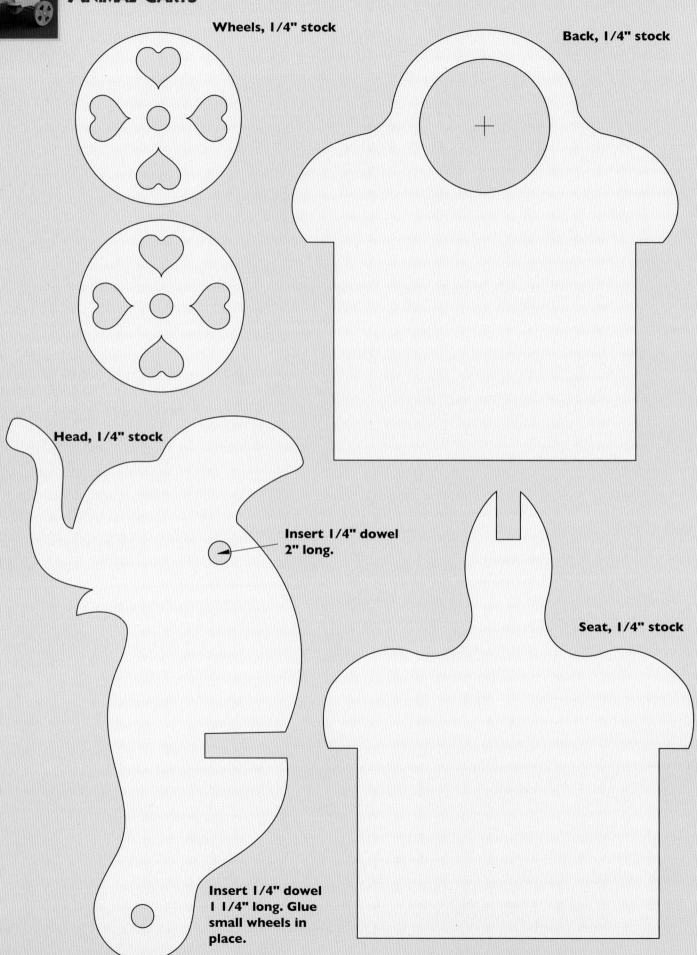

Rocking Bench

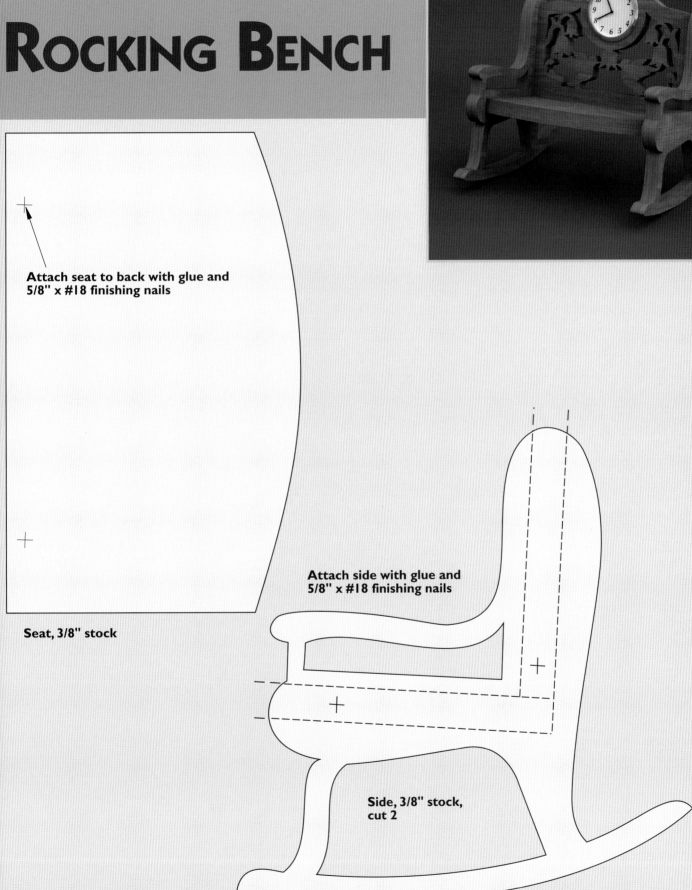

Attach seat to back with glue and
5/8" x #18 finishing nails

Seat, 3/8" stock

Attach side with glue and
5/8" x #18 finishing nails

Side, 3/8" stock,
cut 2

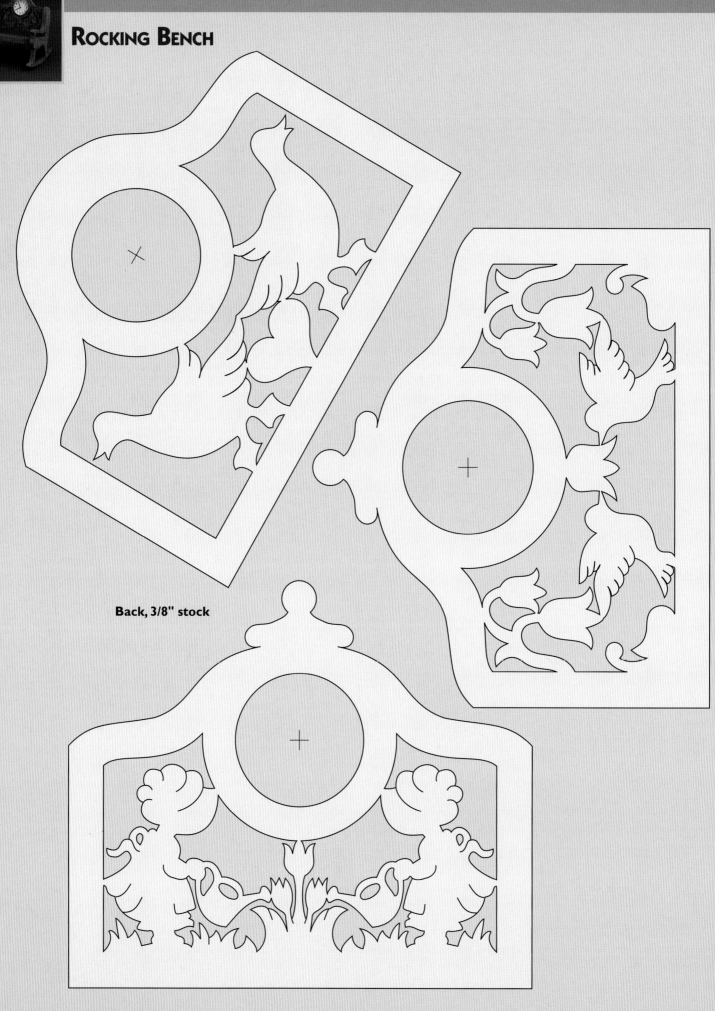

Rocking Bench

Back, 3/8" stock

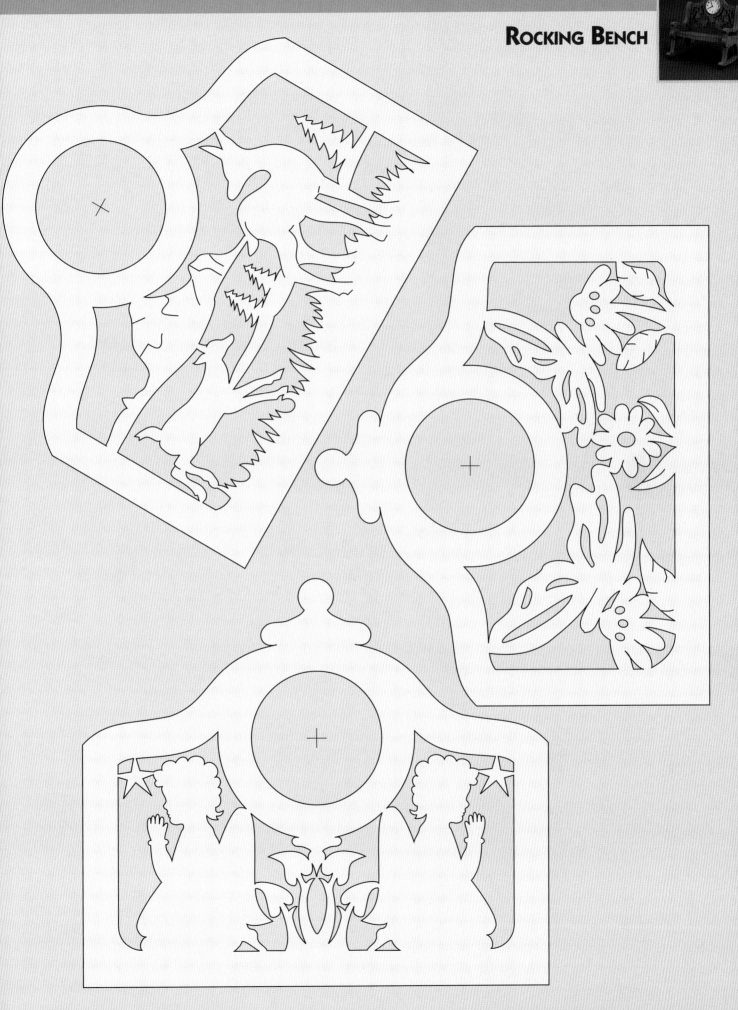

BASES

Attach base to rockers with glue and #18 x 5/8" finishing nails.

Base, I/4" or 3/8" stock

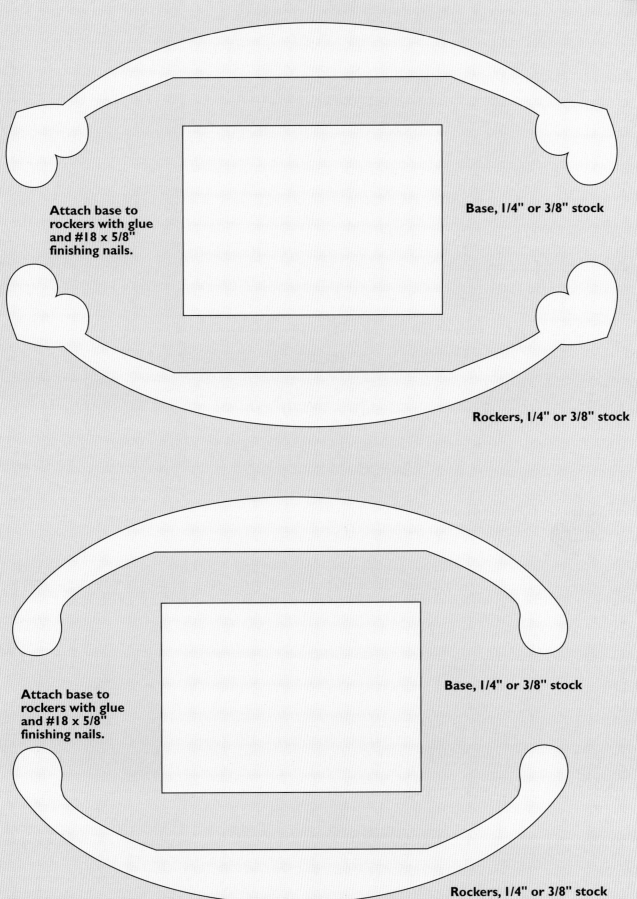

Attach base to rockers with glue and #18 x 5/8" finishing nails.

Base, 1/4" or 3/8" stock

Rockers, 1/4" or 3/8" stock

Attach base to rockers with glue and #18 x 5/8" finishing nails.

Base, 1/4" or 3/8" stock

Rockers, 1/4" or 3/8" stock

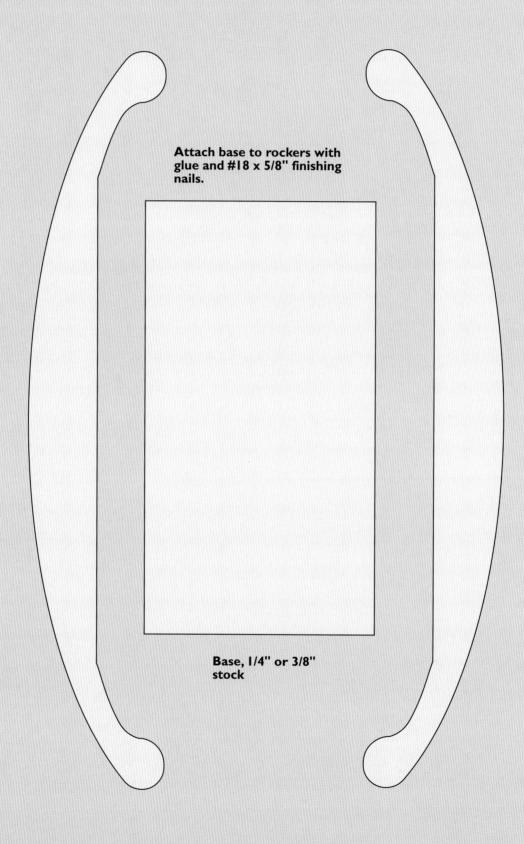

Attach base to rockers with glue and #18 x 5/8" finishing nails.

Base, 1/4" or 3/8" stock

Stock, 3/4"

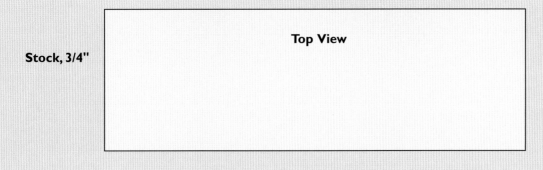

Top View

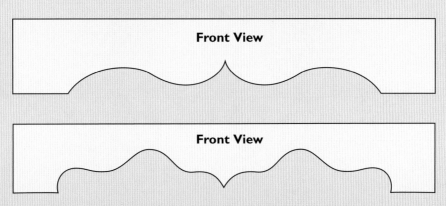

Front View

Front View

Cut the workpiece to size according to the top view dimensions. Adhere the front view pattern to the front of the workpiece. Proceed by turning the workpiece onto its side with the decorative pattern face up. Then, cut along the solid outside line.

Top View

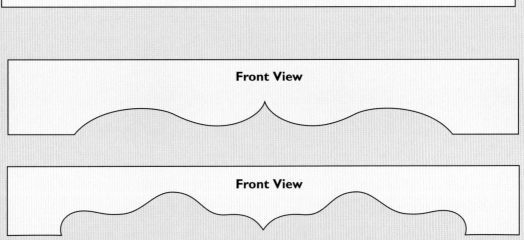

Front View

Front View

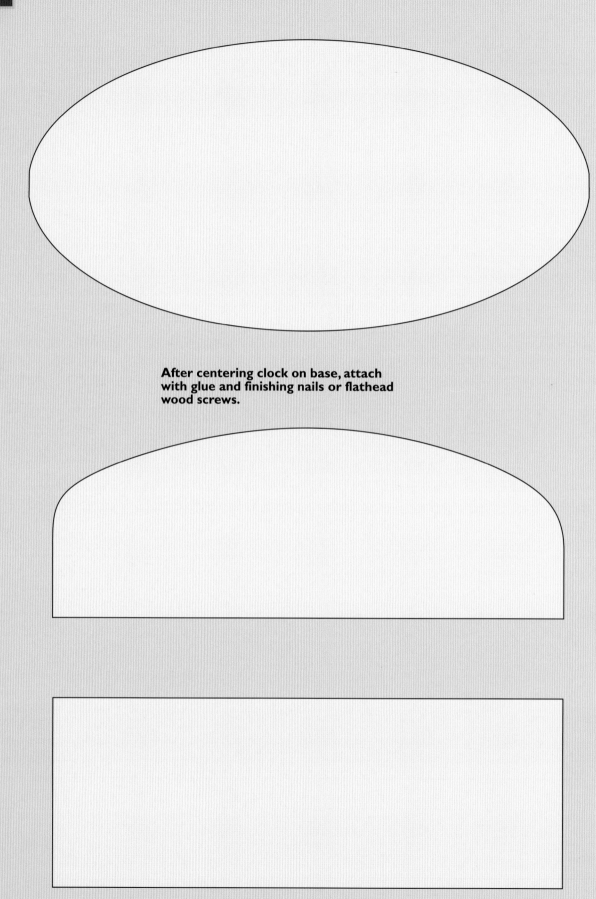

After centering clock on base, attach
with glue and finishing nails or flathead
wood screws.

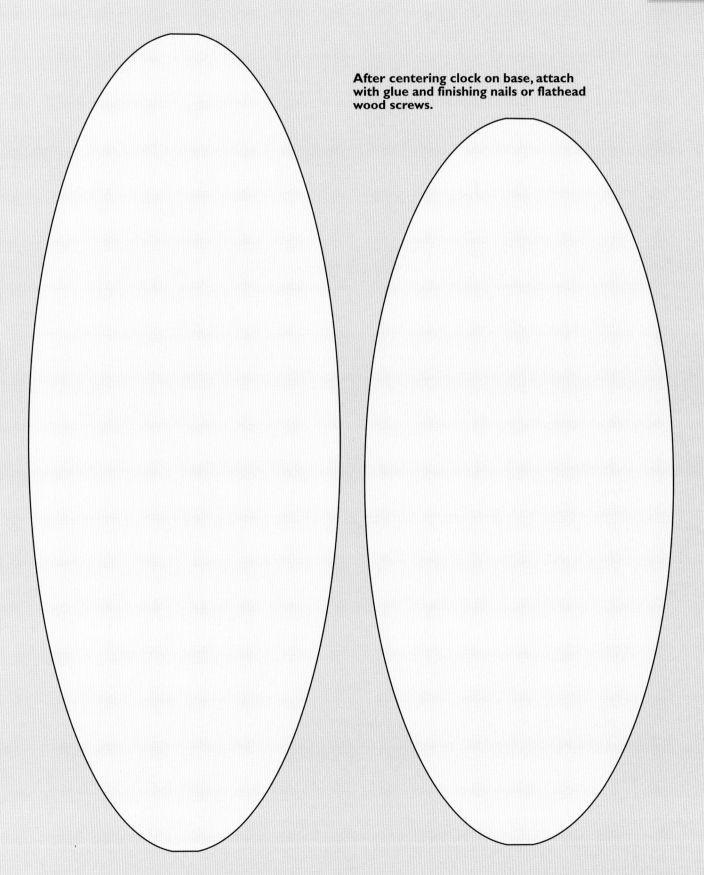

After centering clock on base, attach
with glue and finishing nails or flathead
wood screws.

BASES

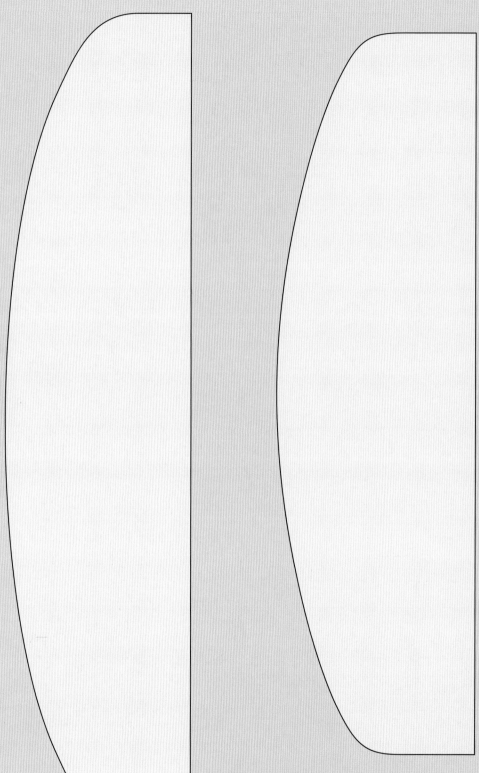

After centering clock on base,
attach with glue and finishing nails
or flathead wood screws.

After centering clock on base,
attach with glue and finishing nails
or flathead wood screws.

More Great Project Books from Fox Chapel Publishing

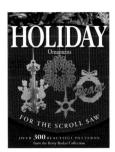

Holiday Ornaments for the Scroll Saw
Over 300 Beautiful Patterns from The Berry Basket Collection
by Rick and Karen Longabaugh
Price: $16.95
Soft Cover
ISBN: 1-56523-276-3
Pages 120
8.5" x 11"

Scenes of North American Wildlife for the Scroll Saw
25 Projects from The Berry Basket Collection
by Rick and Karen Longabaugh
Price: $16.95
Soft Cover
ISBN: 1-56523-277-1
Pages 120
8.5" x 11"

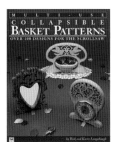

Multi-Use Collapsible Basket Patterns
Over 100 Designs fc the Scroll Saw
by Rick and Karen Longabaugh
Price: $12.95
Soft Cover
ISBN: 1-56523-088-4
Pages 128
8.5" x 11"

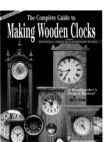

Complete Guide to Making Wooden Clocks 2nd edition
by John A. Nelson
Price: $19.95
Soft Cover
ISBN: 1-56523-208-9
Pages 184
8.5" x 11"

Compound Scroll Saw Creations
Ready-to-Cut Patterns and Techniques for Clocks, Candlesticks, Critters and More
by Diana Thompson
Price: $14.95
Soft Cover
ISBN: 1-56523-170-8
Pages 72
8.5" x 11"

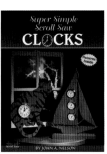

Super Simple Scr Saw Clocks
by John A. Nelson
Price: $9.95
Soft Cover
ISBN: 1-56523-111-2
Pages 64
8.5" x 11"

LOOK FOR THESE BOOKS AT YOUR LOCAL BOOK STORE OR WOODWORKING RETAILER

Or call 800-457-9112 • Visit www.FoxChapelPublishing.com

Learn from the Experts

Fox Chapel Publishing is not only your leading resource for woodworking books, but also the publisher of the two leading how-to magazines for woodcarvers and woodcrafters!

WOOD CARVING ILLUSTRATED is the leading how-to magazine for woodcarvers of all skill levels and styles—providing inspiration and instruction from some of the world's leading carvers and teachers. A wide range of step-by-step projects are presented in an easy-to-follow format, with great photography and useful tips and techniques. *Wood Carving Illustrated* delivers quality editorial on the most popular carving styles, such as realistic and stylized wildlife carving, power carving, Santas, caricatures, chip carving and fine art carving. The magazine also includes tool reviews, painting and finishing features, profiles on carvers, photo galleries and more.

SCROLL SAW WORKSHOP is the leading how-to magazine for novice and professional woodcrafters. Shop-tested projects are complete with patterns and detailed instructions. The casual scroller appreciates the in-depth information that ensures success and yields results that are both useful and attractive; the pro will be creatively inspired with fresh and innovative design ideas. Each issue of *Scroll Saw Workshop* contains useful news, hints and tips, and includes lively features and departments that bring the world of scrolling to the reader.

Want to learn more about a subscription? Visit **www.FoxChapelPublishing.com** and click on either the *Wood Carving Illustrated* button or *Scroll Saw Workshop* button at the top of the page. Watch for our special **FREE ISSUE** offer! You can also write to us at 1970 Broad Street, East Petersburg, PA 17520 or call toll-free at 1-800-457-9112.